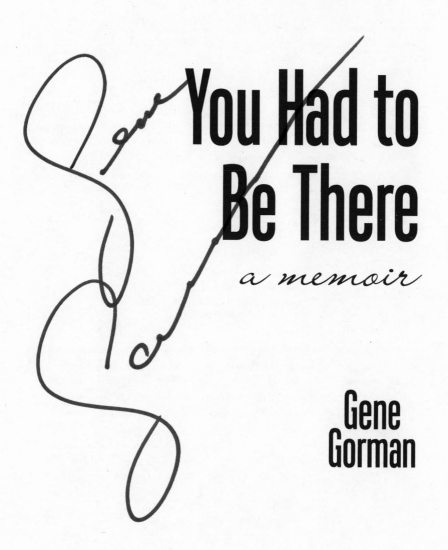

You Had to Be There

a memoir

Gene Gorman

ARCHWAY
PUBLISHING

Archway Publishing books may be ordered through booksellers or by contacting:

Archway Publishing
1663 Liberty Drive
Bloomington, IN 47403
www.archwaypublishing.com
1-(888)-242-5904

ISBN: 978-1-4808-1111-9 (sc)
ISBN: 978-1-4808-1113-3 (hc)
ISBN: 978-1-4808-1112-6 (e)

Library of Congress Control Number: 2014917777

Printed in the United States of America.

Archway Publishing rev. date: 10/15/2014

Contents

preface

It seems unusual that I would be writing a book about anything considering I don't know how to type, was not a great student and by all reasonable estimates shouldn't even be alive, let alone be asked to tell others about my somewhat successful life journey.

There has always been a part of me that felt my story in book form could be of some interest and value to others, but then I thought, *Maybe that's just my ego talking.* The truth is I've often been as surprised as anyone else that I'm alive and have enjoyed considerable success. In fact, I've always thought that if I could be successful, even with my life experiences, anybody can be successful. Ego or not, once I got started, it was only with the constant urging of peers, friends, and family that I finally got motivated to finish putting my story on paper. If nothing else, I thought, at least I can leave a little history for my family, perhaps answering the question "What was wrong with Grandpa Gorman, anyway?"

The ground rules for me were to be as honest as I know how to be and present my story in the language of the times—sometimes gruff but always as it was. I've also tried to present the facts of each "adventure" as I perceived them, understanding that my view of things has become clearer after thirty-seven years of living without alcohol and with a rigorous, albeit imperfect, daily discipline of prayer and showing up where I'm supposed to be when I'm supposed to be there.

As usual, action was the key, so as I hunted and pecked my way through writing this book, I was left with the one absolute that seems to have held me in good standing in a results-based world: "Education is a valuable asset, but what you do is more important than what you know how to do."

The cafeteria was filled that night as I was about to be discharged from the state mental hospital's Alcohol Treatment Unit (ATU). Every Friday, Dr. Petersen, the head internal medicine doctor would have a bon voyage–type farewell for the patients who were going to be leaving. Before being discharged, patients would have to share with the others what they were going to do differently to ensure that they stayed sober. They would usually talk about going to certain twelve-step meetings and changing friends or housing, which was always followed by "making sure I take my Antabuse every day."

Dr. Petersen was a good and patient doctor who had saved many lives with his compassion for treating alcoholics. Most doctors would just give them some tranquilizers and write them off. You can't really blame them, for honesty is a missing piece in the world of active alcoholics, and who wants to deal with people they can't trust? It takes a special doctor who understands addiction and has realistic expectations.

Antabuse is a drug that recovering alcoholics take with the knowledge that they will become violently ill and perhaps even die if they drink while it is in their system, so the logical brain would say, *Don't drink*. It is strongly encouraged by the good doctor, and almost everyone commits to taking it before they are discharged. In fairness, it has worked to buy a little time for some before they take that first drink, but usually it is not a long-term solution. In my case it wasn't even a consideration. I did not plan to take it, and I let the doctor know.

Before long, it was my turn to be put on the spot in front of the entire group of perhaps fifty to sixty people. As usual, I had tried to become the coolest guy in the mental hospital, and since I was a veteran of this particular unit, I felt I was somewhat of a celebrity as far as detoxes were concerned. In fact, there was still a piece of my pottery on the wall from my previous hospitalization's art therapy class. "Michelangelo has returned," I proudly proclaimed upon entering the door for my second visit, to the raised heads of the other "nuts" in the unit, before falling over the dayroom sofa and passing out.

It's a thin line that runs between alcoholics and the mentally ill. All I know is that a drunken alcoholic looks the same as most drunken mental patients. There were certainly no babies being born in this hospital.

Since it was my second time around the ATU, Dr. Petersen had tried hard to convince me to take the Antabuse, all to no avail. I guess he felt he would try to embarrass me into taking it as a last resort. He said, "Now, members of the community,"—he liked that better than *patients*—"we have one of our repeat members, Gene, who is about to be discharged, who refuses to take Antabuse, and this is his second time here. Perhaps he would be willing to share with the other members of the community why he refuses to take it." I sat silently for a moment, eyeballing the audience and at the same time relishing the attention, and then I spoke. "Dr. Petersen, with all due respect, you may be the only person in this room who doesn't know why I refuse to take Antabuse," and then I sat down. Within two days, I was back on the street, stealing wine and asking myself, *How did I get so screwed up when I had so much promise?*

chapter 1

How It All Started: A Little Family History

Eugene J. Gorman and Marion Frances Turner, my dad and mom, met in New York when they were both in the Navy. She was a medical corps WAVE, and he had been decorated at Pearl Harbor during the bombing, so they had a lot to talk about. They dated briefly, about six weeks, and fell in love. They were married in 1943. This would be considered record time in modern times, but it was not so unusual back then. The war was on, and they were caught up in the baby boomers' "generation building campaign." They were pretty good at it too.

I was born in Brooklyn, New York, on September 5, 1946. My father was stationed there in the US Navy. I had a sister, Pat, who was about fourteen months older than me. Mom assumed the task of homemaker while Dad went to sea.

We moved quite often during those first few years. Pat was born in Philadelphia, and then it was on to New York, followed by Wisconsin; Jacksonville, Florida; Portsmouth, Virginia; and then back to Philadelphia, where my sister Mary was born. All this moving was done out of naval training necessity in a span of about three years. The other three kids in our family—Phil, Nina, and Susan—were born in Norfolk and Virginia Beach, Virginia, which is basically where we all grew up.

Dad loved the Navy. They gave him specific directions on how to live, what to do, and when to do it. Perhaps out of necessity, that was to remain a strong part of his philosophy throughout his life—just tell me what to do and I'll do it. He also seemed to do it better than most of his peers, evidenced by his going from a high school dropout to a commissioned officer. One of the many philosophies I would learn from him was the "just show me what to do" one.

Dad had been raised along with his sister, Mabel, by his grand-parents. His mom, May Belle Hinton, had died at twenty-six when he was an infant, and his dad, Owen, was doing a lot of boozing, so the family felt "the kids will be better raised in a more stable environment." This was a challenging proposition considering that the grandparents were already raising ten of their own children. His grandpa was somewhat of an alderman for the New York Irish community and had a house on the hill; he ran a pretty tight household. Grandma made sure everyone wore dress clothes to dinner and that the boys wore knickers, grace was said, and that was that.

*

Mom was Dad's princess. She was the first woman who really swept him off his feet. What's not to love? She was drop-dead gorgeous, was a terrific dancer, played the piano, and had a per-sonality unmatched by anyone he had ever met. She also had that little touch of class he had become accustomed to in his upbringing. Her dad, William Owen Turner, had been a college boy and a successful insurance salesman. Her mom, Nina, saw herself as somewhat of an aristocrat. She would play the piano during the Depression and sing to the homeless and unemployed as she served them sandwiches while they sat on her porch, I'm sure raising the eyebrows of some of the neighbors because they lived in a pretty nice neighborhood. That didn't matter to "Nana," though; she was on a mercy mission.

Sadly, Mom's dad died of a heart attack at the age of fifty, at the peak of his career. Suddenly the world was turned upside down for both her and Nana.

Mom was dealing with the challenges of moving all over the place, raising children, and doing most of it alone since Dad was out to sea most of the time. It was also around then that Mom started experiencing tremendous anxiety and started having panic attacks. As the story goes, she was seeing a psychiatrist at the time, and between visits she would often have to swoop up Pat and me and bolt out the door for an emergency visit. I personally believe she started medicating herself with a few drinks to help hold things together, waiting for Dad to come back from sea or work or wherever he might be at the time.

The nighttime drinking became a regular habit of hers throughout the next twenty-five years, the raising-of-the-children years. When Dad was home from sea, they would go out some evenings to the Officer's Club functions. By that time, it was obvious that she had no control once she started drinking. Her personality would really shine, and Dad loved it. Then it would go a little too far, and on more than one occasion Mom brought a little too much attention to the rising young naval officer. He was advised to get his wife under some sort of control. Good luck with that.

While my father was the image of correctness and stability, Mom was the personality of the entire family, and we were all caught up in her world of anxious existence. Dad would go out to sea, and Mom would start spending the household money on drinking. With a bunch of kids in the picture, it wasn't long before we all started realizing that we had no money. Looking back at those years, it seems now that they were the most important years of my life and helped establish a work ethic that would stay with me forever.

chapter 2

1952: The Early School Years

My recollection of my early school years is a bit vague, but I do remember elementary school, and in the first grade, at a manly six years old, I developed a crush on a pretty little girl named Dorothy Bradshaw. Of course, I never had the courage to tell her. It might have had something to do with her dad. He was the caretaker for Forest Lawn Cemetery, and they lived on the grounds, which freaked me out a bit. My first-grade teacher, Mrs. Redman, played an important role in my life. First of all, she was beautiful, and perhaps more important, she really got our class into reading. For some reason, I was pretty good at it. Baseball quickly became my favorite sport and by the fourth grade I was devouring all the baseball books I could read. My first claim to fame was when my fourth grade teacher, Mrs. Wiggins, had our book reports put in the local paper, and mine, along with my picture was one of the featured ones. Beautiful and brilliant Mrs. Redman had no idea what she was starting.

*

As a result of Dad's military jobs and our growing family, I changed schools frequently in those early years. I went to a different school each year from first through sixth grade. In fact, in the fifth grade, we were bused from our Norfolk neighborhood to a Virginia Beach school some fifteen miles away because of the integration stance taken by the Norfolk schools. They had chosen to close the schools rather than integrate. Of course, we kids had no idea why we were bused; we just thought it was cool to take that long bus ride each morning.

In those early school years, I also discovered that I was a pretty good athlete. At recess I was always one of the fastest guys and seemed to excel at all of the sports being taught, so when it was time to try out for some of the local recreation and Little League teams, I had no problem making the team. Of course, I wanted to be involved in every play, so I chose to become a catcher. I loved it. I was a constant chatterbox and was able to direct the team from my unique position, where I could see everything. I usually made the All-Star teams and was often chosen as the most valuable player. As fate would have it, once I was in high school, sports would be out of the question.

With our family's financial condition, I needed to work after school each day. I remember being envious as I saw many of my friends and former teammates go on to excel in high school sports with all of the accolades and scholarships available to good athletes, and I always felt a bit left out in the cold because I knew my talent level.

This frustrated me a great deal, but it was just the way it was. I soon discovered that we all shine at different times and in different places in our lives, and it just wasn't my time.

When I was in the seventh grade, attending Larrymore Elementary School, two major events happened: I got my first girlfriend, Gwen Hall, and I got into my first fight with a bully. It seems Paul Condell was a bit jealous of my having this good-looking girlfriend, and he put me into a position where I had to defend my honor and unfortunately defend it in front of the entire school. The only thing I can say is that I initially avoided the confrontation—primarily because he was a big, big kid and would have embarrassed and hurt me. Unfortunately, as is the case with most bullies, he continued to challenge me publicly until, after about a week of this daily abuse—we walked home on the same route—I felt I had had enough. I walked up to him and said, "Let's do it." After I initially kicked him in the groin to try and even the playing field, he commenced to put a little ass whipping on me. However, an interesting thing happened. I found out that I could take a little pain and learn from it, and for the next few days as he continued to challenge me in front of everybody, I started getting closer to winning the battle. Then came that one special day when I said, "Let's do this thing" and he said no. Many years later, after he and I both returned home from Vietnam, he became a good friend and still is.

Now back to my girlfriend. Gwen was absolutely the best-looking twelve-year-old girl in the school. She was madly in love with me, and I was madly in love with her. I would stop at her house on my way home, and we would neck and breathe heavy and I would try to take liberties and she would say no and I would try again and she would say no again, and we would fall more madly in love. All of this was done while her mom was upstairs.

Of course, we would talk about all the things young lovers talk about. This went on throughout the school year, but looming in the distance was the transfer of her father, Major Hall, USMC, to San Diego, California.

As my seventh-grade year wound down, there were a few subjects I seemed to excel at and a few that were a struggle. The ones with the least homework were my favorites, but I really enjoyed English and history. I was a pretty good student, but I had a difficult time staying on task once I was home; that cost me when it came to the grades. By that time in my young life, I had started developing the attitude that I would do whatever I could to just get by, as well as get away with. Whether or not this was some sort of acting out defiantly or whatever would have to be left up to the shrinks later on. There would be plenty of them.

In spite of my defiance, one major occurrence happened around this time in my academic life. Dad had bought us a set of encyclopedias and along with it came a set of books on twenty-four famous American men and women when they were young. They were biographies of people like George Washington, Abraham Lincoln, Clara Barton, George Washington Carver, and so on.

Even though my homework wasn't getting done, I would sit in my room and devour these books. Looking back, I see that as a pivotal period in my life. I gained tremendous confidence by reading their stories, and in spite of the chaos at home sometimes, I felt like, *If they can do it, so can I.*

chapter 3

Eight Years Old:
Time to Get a Job

It was also obvious early on in my growing-up years that money was going to be an issue. With Mom's being a boozer and Dad's being gone most of the time, there was never any money to be had. Mom was always trying to do what was right, but with her drinking, her priorities changed daily.

When I was eight years old, we lived in Norfolk, Virginia, in a slightly lower-middle class neighborhood full of mostly Navy families. I believe in an effort to do the right thing, Mom steered me toward a group of Cub Scouts, thinking they might afford me a little stability and companionship. Most of the guys had uniforms and all the other Cub Scout "stuff," and I remember feeling a little envious. But I knew that with our lack of money, I wouldn't be getting a Cub Scout uniform.

I had already learned that's the way it was when you don't have any money. As fate would have it, one of the scouts subscribed to a magazine entitled *Boys Life*, and I would read it whenever visiting him. The stories were great, but what caught my eye were the advertisements in the back. Some company was paying money for young guys like me to sell Christmas cards door to door and would pay something like 10 percent of the price to the sales guy. It suddenly dawned on me that I could make some money and not have to rely on whatever we could scrape by with from Dad's monthly check that he sent to Mom. At that time, we were putting cardboard in the bottoms of our shoes when the soles wore out and living off of peanut butter and mayonnaise sandwiches for lunch when we went to school. They were not bad once in a while but were becoming pretty regular.

I'll never forget when my first box of cards came in. I tore open the box eagerly and was overwhelmed at this new opportunity to become a "salesman." Off I went knocking on doors and taking orders. It never crossed my mind that I should give up just because a few folks slammed doors in my face. I remember that the directions said it was a numbers game and that success was based on the "law of averages"—whatever that was—so I shouldn't take rejection personally. I never did. Soon, I was bringing home a few bucks and was even loaning money to Mom as she waited for her check "from your father." Her inability to pay me back when I asked created some anger in me, but after she threatened a few times to kill herself because I was ungrateful for all she was doing, I quit asking for repayment and decided to just get a second job. The shrinks and I would discuss this later.

Mom was a talented, beautiful woman, but obviously she was getting sicker from the drinking and the other stresses in her life. I just started backing away from the house as much as possible and sort of became an isolated young business guy. In fact, when I wasn't at school or working, I would hide out in an old car behind the house or sneak into the movie theater down the road. In those days, I would do anything to stay away from the house.

I went back to my friend's *Boys Life* magazine to search for another job. I spotted a real cool-looking ad of a young guy who was selling *Grit* on street corners, and that caught my interest. *Grit* was old news that had already been in the local papers, but boys could sell it for a nickel while standing on a corner at stoplights as the cars drove by. The company kept half, and the boys kept half. Sales boys had to be twelve or thirteen to have a regular paper route and had to have a bike, and I didn't qualify either way. So I kept doing this type of free-styling stuff and sold magazines door to door when the seasons would change. I just seemed to be driven to make a few bucks for myself and knew there was no money for me from any other sources. This type of youthful entrepreneurship went on for the next couple of years. Before long we had moved to a bigger house to accommodate our growing family. By 1959 we had six children. I guess you could say we had reached our Catholic quota because the kids stopped coming after that.

After moving into our bigger house I had a variety of jobs over the next few years. They included lawn cutting, baby-sitting, delivering papers, and of course selling my cards and other items door to door.

*

As mentioned, flexibility was very important to me because I was playing sports as well as going to school. It was at this time that my dad felt I should start paying room and board, saying that half of the money from my jobs should go to Mom for my rent. My dad only knew that we were broke and that I could help. He was just trying to pay the bills and keep everyone clothed and fed. The dynamics of a large family in which one of the parents is an alcoholic are interesting. Those involved learn some very valuable survival instincts.

This type of work balance would stay with me throughout all of my junior high and high school years. I do not remember ever asking or getting any money from my parents.

chapter 4

1958: Real Sex and Raymond Johnson

When we were twelve or thirteen, a few buddies of mine and one of their sisters, who was fifteen, were hanging out in our neighborhood at this old tree swing one Saturday afternoon. We would often play a game at parties called Slap, Kiss, or Hug. One person would stand behind a member of the opposite sex and hold their hand to their lips or cheek or across their chest, and the person in front would guess what their partner was going to get to do to them. Even though we weren't at a party, we decided—at the older sister's urging—to play the game. It seemed harmless enough, but someone changed the title of the game to Slap, Kiss, or Screw. Hell, we didn't really know what screwing was.

In fact, up to that point, all of us were a bit in the dark as to what sex really was all about, but we knew that our buddy wasn't going to kiss or screw his own sister. So we drew straws and, yes, I was the last guy. Kissing and slapping had already been done, so I had to make a decision. At the sister's request, we went to her house and, with her mom in the kitchen, back to her bedroom, and I lost my virginity. I had never had an orgasm before and was scared to death that she would get pregnant. She reassured me that if that happened, she would blame someone else. I went home a bit shaken up and tried to put on a composed face, but it was all to no avail. I felt guilty and scared. In fact, when it came to sex, those two emotions would stay with me for many years.

At dinner that night as the family was eating, I had to excuse myself and burst into tears while running to my room. My dad came back and asked what was wrong, and I told him everything. To his credit, there was no judging—only reassurance that she would probably be okay. He suggested that I probably wasn't the first one to be with her and said that she could always blame someone else. He then advised that I think before I act in the future, and I did. I was twelve years old, and although there was some petting with my future girlfriends, I didn't have sex again until I was married. I'm not sure why, but I often think about President Bill Clinton's well-known statement when I tell this story: "I did not have sex with that woman."

As mentioned earlier, my real love would have been to play sports in school, but circumstances prevented that. I did have a lot of pent-up anger about this issue, and it would stay with me for some time. However, for some magical reason, my self-esteem was intact. Armed with the courage from my previous jobs and historical readings of the famous Americans, my personality was always in high gear. I never once doubted I could be successful at whatever I wanted to do.

I really believe that my value system was established by how I grew up. Coming from a financially challenged environment made me sensitive to others who had to overcome hard times. The famous American books made me see that most leaders had to overcome many obstacles in their young lives. I saw men and women, white and black, persevere and in spite of prejudice and ridicule, stay the course, and become successful.

I never had any problem with prejudice, and it has served me well. In fact, for whatever reason, I always felt a responsibility to help those who were being persecuted. I guess I had some of my grandmother in me. A good example and perhaps a bit of comic relief regarding my attitude is exemplified by my Raymond Johnson story.

Raymond Johnson was a classmate of mine in the eighth grade. The eighth grade is a tough year for all of us because of the coming-into-manhood stuff that's going on and all that jockeying for dominance that seems to go with it. Raymond also had the unfortunate challenge of being gay at a time when it was referred to as being "queer." In addition, he had been cursed with the worst case of acne that I ever saw. He was fifteen and should have been in high school, but he had been held back because his folks had felt it best in his early years. As a result of these unavoidable problems, he was the target of extreme ridicule and bullying from just about everyone in class.

Gym class was horrifying for him. He was always the last one in and first one out, if he attended at all. Understandably, I never remember him taking a shower. I was generally accepted by everyone as a result of standing up to one of the school bullies during the first week I was at that school and excelling at sports during class. I'm not sure why, but for some unexplainable reason I felt the need to defend him from all the other kids. Cruelty and prejudice just drove me crazy. I would make it a point to be kind to him and protectively walk with him out of gym class.

One day as we were leaving class, he told me his mom was going to let him drive her car around the neighborhood and asked if I would like to have him pick me up. He even said he would let me drive. Of course I said yes. I think he was just trying to show his gratitude for the kindness I had been showing him. Now, I couldn't tell my parents because I wasn't old enough to drive, but what the heck. I was thirteen and a half years old, so this was a big deal to me.

About five thirty that evening, he came by my house and I met him out front. As we were driving around, he showed me a few things I needed to know to drive and then pulled over and asked me if I wanted to give it a try. Yep! Let me at that steering wheel. As I was walking around that big station wagon to the driver's side, I noticed a bunch of grocery bags in the back seat.

I asked, "What's with the groceries?" He responded, "Oh, my mom just didn't take them all inside before I got the car." *Oh, okay.* It made sense to me—sort of. Anyway, off we went.

As I was driving around the neighborhood, I noticed in the rearview mirror that there was a truck following us, and I said to Raymond, "I wonder why that truck is following us?" So I pulled over. He wanted me to step on it, but with my limited experience, I felt it would be best to find out what was going on. When I stopped, the guy in the truck pulled in at a slant in front of us and jumped out of the truck. Raymond reached over, grabbed the keys out of the ignition, bolted out the passenger door, and took off screaming, "Mama!" I sat there bewildered until the guy reached in the window, grabbed me by the collar, and said, "What the fuck are you doing with my car?" Being scared to death, I answered, "This is Raymond's mom's car. Her groceries are even in the back." That didn't go over very well.

He held my collar while the neighbors called the police and the neighborhood cop arrived. We all knew Valley, the cop .He assured everyone that he would get to the bottom of this and that I was basically a good guy, regardless of some of the run-ins we had had before.

As it turned out, Raymond, in an effort to show his gratitude for my kindness, had stolen the car from in front of the local Farm Fresh grocery store while the lady was taking her empty basket back to the store. That's why we had groceries in the back seat.

In fact, Raymond Vaughan may be responsible for stores across America now having specific areas on the parking lot to drop off your basket. I like to think that anyway.

My parents were called, and when my dad showed up, we all got in the cop car and went to Raymond's house to look for him. Although he wasn't home, we met his dad and explained the situation. He seemed like he didn't care and wasn't surprised, and I couldn't help but think how painful it must have been for Raymond growing up.

Strangely enough, I didn't get much more than a little lecture from my dad. He must have realized it was punishment enough just to be in that situation. And we still didn't know what tomorrow would bring.

The next day at school, I was called to the principal's office. The cops were there, and they had me go down with them to point out Raymond, who had surprisingly come to school. They took him away, and I never saw him again. I felt like a traitor to my sense of caring, but I reasoned that life goes on.

chapter 5

1960: The High School Experience

hen it was on to high school. I was not really a good student. However, as usual, I seemed to excel at history and English— and of course PE. Any courses that required a lot of logical thinking but didn't have a lot of emotion in them were my greatest struggles.

I failed algebra twice and sciences were difficult for me, so I switched to business math courses because I had already been in business for years; succeeding at those came easy. Percentages and profit margins I fully understood. I took the science classes in summer school until I passed them ... barely. The courses that had some color held my interest, and I did well in them. In addition, if I could get some recognition while taking them, I really did well.

I got involved in the drama and speech clubs in school and excelled. Since I had to work after school, the clubs were ways for me to get my strokes and, yes, do a little showing off. What the heck—I'd been speaking to strangers in public since I was eight years old. I found out that I loved to act. I could escape into what-ever role I was playing. It was as good as hiding in a car behind the house. I had the male lead in a lot of the school plays—*Don*

Quixote, Picnic, Macbeth, and *The Wizard of Oz.* I was rolling along pretty well and was even voted the Most Talented Student in my senior year high school hall of fame.

I was easily accepted by every group at school and was beginning to feel like somewhat of a celebrity. My drama teacher, Don Vinny, felt confident that he could get me a fine arts scholarship. He mentioned his alma mater, Carnegie Tech, and the Lee Strasberg Theatre and Film Institute in New York City. My hopes rose, but I kind of knew that would never happen.

In my junior year, 1963, I was asked to join the local high school fraternity, Pi Delta Pi, to which Joe Harrell, undoubtedly the coolest guy in school—who is a close friend to this day—and all the other "cool" guys belonged. We would all sit together at the Friday night football games (when I didn't have to work) and drink illegally. There was also a high school sorority that all the cool girls belonged to, and I was starting to keep my eye on one of them. Life was good.

✱

In the midst of all of this good stuff, I was still working and my ego was starting to get "super healthy." I was elected VP of the Distributive Education Club. These were students who went to school half the day and went to work after that.

My day would flow like this: get a ride or hitchhike to work in my tie after school, sell shoes at Russell and Holmes shoe store until 7:00, and then hitchhike to the Boulevard movie theater three miles away, where I had another job as an usher.

The movies were sort of like soft porn and the pay was bad, but it kept me working and away from the house. I would then hitchhike home at about eleven and get ready to go to school the next day.

As you can imagine, homework was not a big priority in my schedule, but the total financial independence that I earned was to become part of my foundation later in life. But there was a lot of adventure to happen before then.

Even though I was accepted as one of the cool guys at school, my home life was still tumultuous. Mom's drinking was getting worse, and the chance of my taking advantage of one of the scholarships was never considered. I remember mentioning it to Mom, and she sadly pronounced that she too could have been something special with her talent if she hadn't had to raise six children. It was part of the drinking that bred this type of self-centeredness. I never brought it up again.

Throughout my junior and senior years, I continued to work and get my strokes from my acting and speaking in school. It was about this time that I started going out on weekends with my buddies who had cars.

Gene Reyes was from the Philippines and had played varsity football for our school. He was one of those guys who hung around with the underclassmen even after he graduated, living off of past glories. We became good friends.

He had a car and knew all of the angles on how to get some wino to buy us some beer, and we could stay at his parents' house for the night because they would be in bed and never knew what was happening. We would go to a teen dance on Saturday nights, and it was at one of those that I went through my first drinking struggles.

I had my first beer at a place called Vito's Bar when I was fifteen. Vito was a little baldheaded guy who could barely see over his bar, but if you had fifteen cents, you could get a 3.2 percent alcohol draft beer. But then we graduated to real beer and sometimes even cheap liquor. After drinking my quart of beer or at least acting like I drank it—I didn't really like the taste—I would go into the teen club and act like I was cool. Of course, I was never as cool as I acted, but I was a good actor so I faked them out. And boy, could I dance.

As was the usual case, I drew a lot of attention because of my behavior, and the crazier I got the more attractive I became to a select group of girls at the dances. I was to find out years later that it's almost magnetic—that psychologically screwed-up women are often magnetically attracted to screwed-up men and vice-versa. It's strange how that works.

chapter 6

Falling in Love

B everly was a cute yet somewhat shy girl with what seemed a high degree of stability in her world. I was attracted to that. She always wore the nicest clothes and was a member of that high school sorority that all the cool girls belonged to. She wore those Weejun loafers and those circle pins on her sweater that meant she was part of the in crowd. I would see her at school and then at the teen club dances, and we were drawn to each other. We danced together and even won a few dance contests. I was anxious to take her out. Unfortunately, I had no car, and my dad would usually only let me drive from three to seven on Sunday afternoons. That's not exactly when everything is "happening."

Understandably, with all of our kids, Mom always wanted a car to be at her disposal, and we only had one car. So Sunday afternoons were it.

Prior to dating Beverly, I met her mom, Kitty, one night when I was down at Virginia Beach with some of my fraternity brothers. They called it house party weekend. It was toward the end of the school year, and the sororities would go down to rent a house, walk the beach, and flirt with the guys for the weekend. Each sorority had a few mothers as chaperones, and Kitty was one of them. We "cool guys" were all boozed up, and as fate would have it, I fell into Kitty's lap while she was sitting on the porch and promptly told her how much I loved "older women." In her gentle way, she assured me that if she was twenty years younger, we might have had a chance. Little did I know that this was Beverly's mother and that much later Kitty told Beverly about this crazy guy she met at the house party over the weekend. I think Kitty fell in love with me right away. It would take a little longer for Beverly.

I'm not sure Beverly fell for me as much as she fell for my popularity and craziness. Whichever it was, it wasn't long before we started seeing each other and dating. It was the summer after my junior year in high school. My close friend, David, was dating Beverly's best friend, Linda, and he had access to a car, so our dates were generally on Friday nights and Sunday afternoons.

Saturday nights were usually reserved for drinking with the guys and seeing Beverly at the teen dances. Standard dating usually concluded with heavy petting as well as driving around looking at expensive houses like the one we planned to buy when we got married.

✳

Beverly was from a modest yet disciplined home. Her stepfather, Clarence, had been raised in a Masonic orphanage and ran the home with a firm hand. He had married Kitty when Bev's dad abandoned the family and, believe it or not, joined the circus. Clarence was a solid breadwinner who had never been married before. He ran a stern, orphanage-type household, and he had taken on Kitty and her daughters; that meant he ran things his way.

I'm quite sure there were a few raised eyebrows as Clarence was adjusting to this crazy guy Kitty's daughter had started dating. They would get even more raised as the years went by.

In a strange sort of way I was falling in love with Beverly, but it wasn't necessarily because of passion. Sure, she was attractive and well groomed, but more important than that, she was stable. I was attracted to that stability, and I felt like she saw me as her knight in shining armor. I was her Don Quixote, and she was my Lady Dulcinea. She wanted out of her rigid, disciplined home and saw me as a way out—by this time, a very interesting way out for sure.

Beverly had been greatly influenced by some of her "old money" type relatives in New Bern, North Carolina. They had nice homes and were members of the country club; life seemed grand for them. Beverly got on a fast track to try to get to that status as soon as possible. Somehow that was also attractive to me. I guess I was still influenced by my grandmother. But we were both only seventeen and still in school. For the time being, we would just have to settle for driving around on Sundays dreaming and trying to endure Clarence until we could get married.

I was often curious about whether Kitty ever told him about our first meeting at the beach house. But Kitty was my biggest fan and would smooth things over between Clarence and me many times in the future.

chapter 7

1964: I Don't Know Where You're Going, but You Can't Stay Here

I n my senior year, it was obvious I wasn't going to be staying at home long after graduation. Dad had already established the rule that once I was out of school, I was to go somewhere. I just couldn't stay home. One less kid to worry about was certainly on his mind, and with my drinking and craziness, it seemed reasonable. He had retired from his beloved US Navy and was now trying to become a successful businessman, husband, and father to the younger members of the family. He believed a young man should be out on his own as soon as possible. I had already been pretty much on my own, but it seemed the "out" part was what he was interested in.

To help prepare for this upcoming change in my life, I thought I had better see what was available for a seventeen-year-old high school graduate.

One afternoon in April of 1964, I went into downtown Norfolk and was walking up and down the Armed Forces recruiter's hall in one of those old, sturdy brick buildings you find in all downtowns. I thought that maybe after high school I would join the service and then go to school or perhaps even stay if I liked it. I already knew a lot about the Navy, so I went to talk to them first. When I walked in the door, I spotted a couple of Navy guys playing cards and drinking coffee. They looked at me and said, "What can we do for you, young man?" I don't know why, but I asked where the Army guys were. They directed me down the hall. When I went through that door, the Army guy seemed happy to see me and said, "Come on in." He then had me sit down and started telling me about all the schools available for me, saying all I had to do was get my mom to sign and on and on. It sounded good, but I said, "I'll get back to you." As I walked farther down the hall, I saw the eagle, globe, and anchor of the US Marine Corps. I peeked around the corner, and when I did, this booming voice said, "Come in if you are interested in becoming a marine." I slowly entered, and sitting as straight as an arrow at this huge oak desk was this flat-topped sergeant dressed in the sharpest-seamed shirt, tightest-tied tie, and bluest blue trousers I had ever laid my eyes on. As I tried to get my cool voice on, I asked, "What kind of schools do you guys have available in the US Marines?" He stared directly at me for what seemed like forever and then abruptly stood up.

I was not sure what he was going to do. As he walked out from behind the desk, he slowly headed over to a wall locker, looked to his left, and then looked right into my eyes. Holding my mesmerized gaze, he yanked the precision latch up, exposing a US Marine helmet, an M-14 rifle, and a complete and tightly rolled pack with attached canteen. "This is the school I offer. If you can make it through boot camp, you get to call yourself a marine. Go talk to your folks, or the Air Force is right down the hall. They got all kinds of schools."

That night I told my mom I wanted to be a marine. It was the 120-day delay program, and after getting sworn in a week later,

I wouldn't be going away to Parris Island for boot camp until August. All I needed was someone to sign the parental approval because I was still only going to be seventeen when I went away. She signed the papers and seemed to be very proud of my decision, even though her world was in tough shape once again. Her drinking was getting worse, and Dad had recently completed treatment for melanoma. He was in a good recovery state, but it tended to throw the family a bit more out of whack, what with the big *C* word being used.

The next four months consisted of a little bit of school, a lot of work, and a lot of weekend drinking, with the usual Sunday afternoon dreaming as Beverly and I awaited graduation and my departure for the marines. It was obvious that my parents' pride in their son was coupled with an anxious anticipation of his departure. In fact, Dad even allowed me to use the car one night to go down to the beach, but sadly he had to come bail me out for speeding and driving with no shoes on.

In fact, I got stopped again that same night on the way home and was given another speeding ticket, but this time the cop just got me for speeding because I had put my buddy's shoes on. I never mentioned this second ticket before I left. My dad didn't find out until the police came to the house to arrest me for failing to show for court. He told me years later, "I told the cop you were at Parris Island marine boot camp if they wanted to go get you. They told me they would tell the judge and they were sure he would drop the charges if that was the case."

It was obvious by then that I was starting to enjoy the drinking a bit more than I used to, but with no car of my own, it wasn't getting me into too much trouble other than when I would get dropped off drunk by my friends late and go right to my room. I had always shared a room with Phil, who was now eleven years old. He would sometimes look at my late-night homecomings with caution. I had already thrown up in my bed while drunk one night and then stumbled over and threw up on him in his bed. When he got up, he went upstairs to tell Mom I had thrown up on him, and she told him to just go down and get in my bed until the morning. Of course, he wasn't aware of my previous upheaval in my own bed, so back upstairs he went, where I think she advised him to just work it out somehow. "He'll be leaving to go in the marines soon, and you'll have your own room." That seemed to be the mentality surrounding my bizarre behavior for those last four months—"He'll be going away soon." What a classic understatement that was.

chapter 8

Send in the Marines

My mom took me to the train station in Richmond, Virginia, on August 24, 1964. The train started picking guys up somewhere in the north, probably Maine, and stopped all along the way until we got to Yemassee, South Carolina, where we had a one-night stopover before boarding a bus at about four o'clock in the morning to take us to Parris Island (PI) some twenty miles away. By the time we got to Yemassee, we had about sixty guys. I am convinced that the guy who ran the Yemassee stopover was a former drill instructor who had been demoted for being a sadist psycho. That one night helped prepare us for entry into marine boot camp. Yelling, screaming, and punching in the solar plexus were standard once we got to PI.

Parris Island, South Carolina—the East of the Mississippi, home of the United States Marine Corps Boot Camp—is reputedly the toughest basic training locale of any of the military branches. There is also a boot camp training base in San Diego, California, but all the PI marines considered them "Hollywood Marines." They didn't have to deal with the heat and bugs and overall feeling of being trapped on an island surrounded by quicksand. In fact, a few years earlier, a drunken PI drill instructor had marched his platoon into the swamp late one night and six of them had drowned, further perpetuating the legend of toughness.

As soon as the bus reached its destination on PI, the adventure began. We were taken to the area where all the buses unload, where it was then determined what battalion we would be sent to. We were going to be sent to the 2nd Battalion, affectionately referred to as the Twilight Zone. The 2nd Battalion had the only remaining wooden barracks on the island. We would end up taking great pride in being in that old shantytown and made it a point to rub it in whenever possible to the other two battalions of "candy asses." But that was a few weeks away. When the bus stopped, one of the junior drill instructors boarded it and started the madness instantly. Rush, rush, rush—"Get off the bus! Get off the bus and make two straight lines. Do you know what a straight line is, you stupid motherfucker? Keep your eyeballs straight ahead! Do not say a fucking word because you don't know a fucking thing! Put your feet on the yellow feet, you fucking moron! Are you eye-fucking me, scumbag? Are you queer for me? Do you like me, numb nuts?" *Holy shit*, I thought. *What the hell did I get into?*

We were all as perfectly still as we could be, and out of nowhere appeared our senior drill instructor, Staff Sergeant Cohen. He introduced himself and told us a few of the basics of what would be going on. He was the cool one; the junior drill instructors were the appointed maniacs. Once we were given some basic instructions, by Staff Sergeant Cohen, we were herded toward our new home, but before we got there we were quickly ushered through the process of removing our worthless civilian clothes and putting them in a box to be shipped home. We then walked through another room where we had some basic measurements taken and then were literally thrown our new uniforms and boots, none of which fit.

The first few days were nothing but stark, raging terror for most of us and encompassed the arduous tasks of keeping quiet and doing what we were told. We went through the haircuts, the issuance of basic toiletries, and the navy corpsman with what I swear were shit-eating grins on their faces administering shots in both of our arms as we hurriedly kept moving ahead. We were warned to not stop the line from moving, under penalty of death, it seemed. Once outside, we ran everywhere. They fed us salt tablets all day long. Heat stroke was a big concern but not big enough to keep us from running. The South Carolina swamplands—basically what PI is—get awful hot in August. Pretty soon it became apparent who could walk the straightest, and they were soon made squad leaders. Then came the rest of us, who were still trying to figure out what was right and what was left. "Don't you know right from left, you dumb motherfucker?"

Fortunately, I had been in drama, so I had a little edge on some of the other guys. I could act like I thought they wanted me to and whenever possible really look like a marine recruit. I could put on the "trained killer" look at just the right time. I also was in pretty good shape, so I fared well as we went into the physical aspects of the training. And man, could I march. It was like a military showing-off exercise, and I seemed to be a natural. The drill instructors each barked out commands with their own style of cadence, most of it very colorful, and they were in their element when they were taking us down the drill field, on the way to chow, or wherever we weren't running.

As time went on and we got into the physical elements of training, running, bayonet training, and hand-to-hand combat, I did very well. Before long, I was chosen by Staff Sergeant Cohen to be the platoon guide, a place of honor for any marine recruit. This means that I led the platoon and carried the platoon flag out front just to the right of the senior drill instructor all throughout boot camp. In fact, oftentimes the platoon guide gets promoted to private first class and is the dress blue recruit from the platoon, generally meaning he has the highest overall performance throughout the sixteen weeks of boot camp. In combat units, he is ranked right behind the platoon sergeant in the chain of command. What a cool honor. Once again my ego was starting to shine.

However, I was not top dog in a couple of areas, and they were the ones I could not act my way through. Some of my test scores were a little low when it came to the math and science stuff—not too big of a surprise there. Sadly, there weren't any questions about percentage of profit, but there were a few more in the realm of engineering stuff. This was not my strength. But we did have a guy who scored extremely high, Private Haney. He was chosen to be a Marine Air Recruit Cadet (MARCAD), a recruit who will go into flight school right out of boot camp and become an officer as well as a marine pilot. This is a very big deal to the battalion commander, a lieutenant colonel, who can say he has the only MARCAD from the entire regiment. Unfortunately, Private Haney was a cocky little prick. He was also our first squad leader, a position of rank only behind the platoon guide. Private Haney didn't really like that since he was so much smarter than me, but sadly for him, I excelled in most of the other stuff, particularly the physical stuff like running, hand-to-hand combat, and bayonet training. This animosity would come to a head on the last week of training, but before that, we have to talk about the only guy to my knowledge who ever went drinking while in boot camp at Parris Island.

In my junior year of high school, there was a girl named Kathy Vance who, I guess, had a little crush on me. She was a nice girl, but I had no interest in her other than being a school friend. In fact, her brother and I were fraternity brothers and drinking buddies, and Kathy's dad was also a marine colonel.

Unknown to me, while I was in boot camp, he had been transferred to Beaufort, South Carolina, a marine air base just outside of Parris Island. At about noon on a Sunday in my eighth or ninth week of training, Staff Sergeant Cohen got a call from a General Vance who was at the Hospitality House, and he wanted to see Private Gorman right away.

Staff Sergeant Cohen called me down to the center of the barracks—squad bay, as it was called—and asked, "What the hell does a general want to see you for, scumbag?" I had no idea who it was and certainly didn't know the colonel had become a general. In fact, I hadn't seen Kathy in over six months, so I had really forgotten all about her. I guess you could say I was scared to death. After telling him I didn't know a General Vance, he said I had better get my ass down there right away and not volunteer any information that shouldn't be volunteered. In other words, don't tell the good general that we all get our asses kicked regularly and are verbally abused from morning to night. I bellowed, "Sir! Aye, aye, sir!"

In twenty minutes, I was in my dress uniform and walking down the street toward the Hospitality House. As I came up on the fancy brick building, still wondering who was going destroy my new career so soon, out walked Kathy and one of her hot-looking girlfriends. I almost fell over. She gave me a hug and said, "Come on. Let's go for a ride." It was all against the rules for sure. As I got in the back seat, we started talking and heading for the main gate to leave. I put up a little bit of objection but was reassured by Kathy that the sentry wouldn't stop us because we had a big star on the sticker attached to the bumper. Generals get stars to signify their importance, I guess. When we got to the gate, the marine guard, a lance corporal, I think, looked a bit suspiciously at us three teenagers in the car but snapped to attention and offered a brisk salute. Meekly and staring straight ahead, I returned the salute and out we went.

After driving for about a half mile, we turned into a picnic area on the water, and Kathy broke out a blanket, a Frisbee, and more important, a cooler full of beer. There were also a few "real marines" and their families picnicking and looking at this awkward young recruit, but no one challenged us. We had been sure to park the car with the star pointing toward us. The visit lasted for about two hours and finally, after about four beers, I convinced Kathy to take me back to the base to see if we could sneak me back in.

The whole afternoon was surreal to me, but it gave me a little break in the action and a bit of boasting rights with the guys when I returned to the barracks. When I got back in front of Staff Sergeant Cohen, I assured him that the visit was really with the general's daughter, an old school friend who wanted to tell me how proud her dad was that I chose the marines. I also lied and said the visit took place in a lounge area at the Hospitality House and that everything was handled in a squared-away fashion. I was forever grateful that he didn't get close enough to me to smell my breath. As you can imagine, four beers had me as high as a kite, and the bullshit was flowing freely. To my knowledge and after talking to many fellow marines, I don't know of anyone else who ever went out drinking with a couple of hot babes while they were in Parris Island. Ah yes, drinking opens many doors. Later on, the doors would start closing.

Now we come back to the last week of training and Private Haney. In the sixteenth week of training, everything is pretty much done. We were very close to being called marines, and most of the harassment was over.

Platoon 277 was a fine-tuned, precision team in every area of training. In our platoon, we had accomplished much and were champing at the bit to get on to the next adventure. Most of us were going to be "grunts," meaning that we would in the infantry, and after advanced infantry training we would probably be headed for Vietnam. There were a few who would go on to work in supply, artillery, clerical, cooking, and so on. And then there was Haney. He was the "star" and would soon go on to be an officer and a pilot. These assignments, as well as the dress blue marine and meritorious private first class stripes, would be handed out right after the regimental commander's inspection. Most of the squad leaders and, of course, the platoon guide were the usual candidates for these honors, and we all looked forward to the announcement of who would receive them.

As the platoon guide, one of my duties was to be sure that everybody stayed on task and was doing what they were supposed to while the drill instructor was busy. On the evening before the regimental commander's inspection, we had to clean our rifles to be sure there wasn't a speck of dust on them when the colonel walked the line in front of each squad. Everything had to be perfect.

The usual procedure was the colonel would stop in front of each recruit and look him over. The recruit would come to inspection arms position, open the rifle's chamber, and stand perfectly still. The colonel would then grab the rifle from the recruit, look inside the chamber, and then briskly hand it back to the recruit, who would then smartly place it back on his side while standing at attention.

A dirty rifle would bring the wrath of the drill instructor down on everyone.

To be prepared for this, the evening before the inspection I would call each squad down to the end of the squad bay, and the squad leader would allow each recruit to dip his rifle barrel in the cleaning solvent bucket and then take it back to his rack, sit on his foot locker, and scrub it with a toothbrush until it was clean of any potential rust and dust. The entire bucket routine was supposed to take about fifteen minutes.

Private Haney's first squad would go first. Each squad would get ample time, about five minutes at the bucket. After five minutes, I told Haney to get his squad away from the bucket because we still had two more squads to go. He told me to hold on and that he would move when he was done. This pissed me off, but rather than make a scene I gave him another minute. After that, I walked down to the bucket and told him to get his ass out of the way. He told me to get fucked, and that was about all I needed. Sixteen weeks of maintaining self-control was lost in an instant, and he and I went at it. After stumbling around between racks, I started doing a bit of a punching-bag job on his face and head. By the time Staff Sergeant Cohen broke things up, Haney was in pretty bad shape. He decided he had to send Haney to sick bay for a nose repair and some potential stiches. He then pulled me aside and informed me that my consequences would depend on what Haney said to the doctors at sick bay. Furthermore, if Haney couldn't attend inspection the next day, he didn't know what would happen. Everything depended on what was said at sick bay. It was a long night.

When Haney finally returned from sick bay, it was obvious he wouldn't be able to attend inspection, but to his credit, he used the standard line that he had slipped in the shower. This saved the wrath of the colonel coming down on Staff Sergeant Cohen and his entire command. Unfortunately, I had lost any chance at being the dress blues recruit and wasn't even going to get a stripe because of the incident. I envisioned Haney grinning from ear to ear but was somewhat satisfied that I had done what was necessary to keep my self-respect intact. I always felt that Staff Sergeant Cohen silently endorsed what I had done, evidenced by his maintaining my position of platoon guide throughout the inspection as well as the graduation ceremony. In fact, I was probably the only platoon guide who didn't have a stripe during the ceremony. My parents and Beverly were both at the graduation ceremony, and I was grateful that they never asked about the missing stripe. They just seemed to be typical proud relatives. It wouldn't be the last time my "self-respect" would come with a high price tag.

chapter 9

1965: Training to Be a Killer

After two weeks of leave and spending time with Beverly, plan-
ning our future, it was time to go back to work. It had been
cool, being home and taking in all of the glory that comes with
being a marine. I wore my uniform every chance I had, but now
it was time to get the training that would supposedly prepares
me for combat. Anyone who has ever been in combat knows that
only combat really prepares you. The Infantry Training Regiment
(ITR) at Camp Geiger, in Jacksonville, North Carolina, is where
you get the next best thing.

ITR is where I learned tactics and fired different weapons
as well as mastered the fine points of infantry movement and
assault. This includes tank and other vehicle support strategies.
In the fourth week, we were training on the 3.5 rocket launcher,
sometimes referred to by civilians as a bazooka. We were all in
side-by-side bunkers about four feet high and protected by sand-
bags. The idea is for the loader to insert the rocket into the rear
of the launcher, and then the instructor gives the command for
the shooter to fire. This pause allows the loader to cover his ears.
The blast is very loud and can cause injury if those near it are not
prepared. As we all fired on command, the bunker next to me,
on my right, was late in firing; they fired after I had removed my

hands from my ears. The blast was deafening and left me with a nauseating, high-pitched ringing that I assumed would go away in a few hours. I did all I could to get through the day's training, but as the evening approached I started getting concerned because the ringing never went away.

The next few days of training didn't involve any type of firing or explosive noise, and I continued to hold out hope that I would wake up one morning and the ringing would be gone. The constant ringing coupled with ongoing headaches and a dizzy, nauseating feeling got me worried that there may be a bigger problem than I thought. I held out as long as I could, but I soon became convinced that I needed to go to sick bay and get an evaluation.

The medical doctor checked me out and said I might have some inner ear damage from the 3.5 blast, but his biggest concern was my hearing. He put me in this soundproof room and stated sending different pitches through some earphones he had me wear. Thankfully, I seemed to be able to hear satisfactorily, and he sent me back to work with a "within normal limits" evaluation. Furthermore, he assured me that the ringing would eventually go away. It never did, but, since I loved being a marine, I figured I would just go with it and see what happened. It never dawned on me that the real problem might once again be exacerbated when I was around gunfire or explosive situations. There would be many of them to come in the future.

It was February 1965, and after completing ITR and going home for a couple of more weeks, it was time to go to a more permanent duty station. I was assigned to G Company, 2nd Battalion, 6th Marine Regiment located in Camp Lejeune, North Carolina. The 6th Marines were considered an elite regiment because of fame achieved in World War I at the Battle of Belleau Woods. They were one of two outfits allowed to wear the French Fourregiere, a decorative rope that drapes over the uniform to signify belonging to this unique outfit. It seemed like 6th Marine regimental and battalion commanders drove their units to higher standards of training because of their history. Marines are like that. The rest of us just basked in the pain and glory of "being special."

I'm not sure why or when, but somehow I had gotten a classified security clearance. Staff Sergeant Cohen reasoned that each outfit had to have a certain number of marines get clearances, and since my dad had been career Navy, the investigators would have to go back only one generation to make sure I wasn't a future spy.

During one of our training exercises in the field at Camp Lejeune, a private first class pulled up on a three-wheel Cushman motor scooter and said I had orders to become the Executive Officer's (XO's) driver. He was there to pick me up. This was considered plush duty since it entailed taking care of the major's needs, driving him wherever he wanted to go, and keeping his weapon and other military belongings clean and straight. In addition, I got to drive the XO around when the other guys were marching. It is safe to say that I was not very popular with the rest of the troops in the battalion, but that's strictly because they were envious.

Major Thomas was a bit old to be an XO. He had been passed over three times for promotion, and that meant he was pretty much at his last duty station. I don't think his laid-back style was what they were looking for in the Corps at that particular time. Vietnam was really brewing, and strong commanders were in great demand. The laid-back guys were on their way out.

While I was the XO's driver, the colonel's driver was Sergeant R.D. Williams, a "real marine." Sergeant Williams became my mentor as well as my squad leader.

Every morning he would wake up our squad by yelling, "Get up! Get up, you sons of bitches! Another day to serve the Corps!" We would all moan and groan about his tough demeanor, but secretly we knew he was the best marine in the outfit. He later died in Vietnam doing what he loved to do—being a combat marine.

Most of the noncombat duties were pretty typical for a marine grunt—training in the field Monday through Thursday and having inspections on Friday. On Friday nights, many of us would head home for the weekend. It was easy for me. I only lived four hours away in Norfolk. Mom and Dad let me stay at home on these weekends because they were comfortable that I would be leaving Sunday night. In addition, they seemed to be extremely proud that I was a marine. Some of the guys would drive all the way to Buffalo, New York, spend one night at home, and then turn around and drive back, about fifteen hours each way. It wasn't unusual to hear of these guys having major accidents because they would often fall asleep at the wheel. Some never made it back.

In March of 1965, I bought my first car on one of my weekends at home. It was a 1956 Ford Fairlane with a three-speed gearshift on the column and a 312 cubic-inch V-8 engine. It was a fast and cool-looking car. I paid six hundred dollars for it, and that was a lot of money. At the time I was a private first class and making a whopping ninety-six dollars a month. I had to finance the car with Household Finance Company and pay them thirty-seven dollars a month. As fate would have it, the car had transmission problems from the start. To supplement my income, I used to pick up "marine riders" from the bus stop, and for five dollars each I would drop them off at various towns along the way. Then I would pick them up Sunday night on my way back to the base.

It was a pretty good hustle—for a while. One snowy night in March, all the gears went out on the car except for third. It's very difficult to start off in third gear, so I basically couldn't stop for two hundred miles and had to try to time my drive through each small town so the stop lights wouldn't get me. Somehow we made it, but that was the last trip in my '56 Ford. And I still had to pay on it for the next twenty-seven months. That was one of my first lessons in credit.

Beverly and I decided to get married in December of 1965. We were both nineteen, and in those days that wasn't really that young to get married. I felt that I was in love with Beverly and was motivated by two major reasons to get married: 1) I wanted to be her knight in shining armor and get her away from her dictatorial home life with Clarence, and 2) I thought I would soon be going to Vietnam. I hoped I could get her pregnant and maybe leave a child in case I got killed. Perhaps it was strange how dramatically my brain worked in those days, but surprisingly, it still works along similar lines.

Once the car was gone, I would usually hitchhike home in uniform on Friday night. It was easy to get a ride while in uniform, and I had a lot of experience with hitchhiking from my school days. Dad would let me use the car on Saturday night, and Bev and I would go out with friends or alone. Since we had decided to get married, most of our time was spent driving around dreaming until it was time to go to the local "parking spot" at the airport and neck. On Sunday night, I would take the bus back to the base to be sure I made it back in time for morning inspections.

In June of 1965, the 6th Marines boarded ships at Morehead City, North Carolina, to make our annual three-month Caribbean cruise. We would be doing a whole lot of training and even more partying at various ports of interest in the Caribbean. The island of Vieques, an old US bombing range, was where most of the training was, and the beautiful city of San Juan, Puerto Rico, was where the partying would take place—at least most of it. Before we disembarked and went on our first "liberty," we would all have to listen to a lecture from the gunnery sergeant, who would try to frighten the hell out of us to keep us from going to some of the "low brow" bars in old San Juan. Liberty is when marines are allowed to leave the ship to go into town, with the understanding that we would be back on the ship before muster in the morning.

The "gunny," as he was called, had a strategy. He proceeded to tell us that everyone in the city had the clap or some other VD, as venereal diseases were more commonly refer to. He scared the hell out of me, and I made it a point to go to the fancy Caribe Hilton Hotel in new San Juan. I lost all of my pay in one night at the casino and was back at the ship by about eight o'clock the first evening. The word soon got out that the only one who got VD was the gunny. No wonder he knew the risks so well.

Two days later, we pulled out of San Juan, and after a few days of training in Vieques, we headed to the beautiful Dutch port of Curacao in the Netherlands Antilles. It was there that where we enjoyed our most exciting liberty trip. We went to the Dutch Marine enlisted men's club, and the booze flowed freely. The club was full of marines and sailors from both countries. Tradition called for swapping uniform parts for souvenirs, and by closing time we couldn't tell who was who.

When the big trucks came by to pick us up and take us back to the ship, a herd of strangely uniformed drunk men was going up the gangway and requesting permission to come aboard. We found out later that we pulled out of port with some Dutch Marines on board, and we had to turn the ship around and drop them off at the dock from which we had come. I never heard whether or not anyone got in trouble for that, but it was definitely against regulations.

It was just one more example of booze being a common denominator in trouble. But damn, we had a good time.

Each year all marines are given an option to extend their enlistments and are enticed by the opportunity to name a couple of choices as to where they would like to be stationed next. Since I was starting to really enjoy being a marine with a security clearance, I gave Norfolk as a choice as well as Hawaii, along with perhaps embassy duty in Italy or some other cool place. To further my chances for promotion and for a transfer to one of these spots, I took leadership Marine Corps Institute (MCI) correspondence courses and started to move up in rank. In October of 1965, I was promoted to lance corporal.

chapter 10

Beverly: My First, Second, and Third Wife

O ver the next couple of months, I took on a steady routine of being a marine Monday through Friday till noon and then hitchhiking home on Friday night, waiting for the wedding day, December 4, 1965. Both of our families seemed to be happy about the upcoming marriage. The service was going to be at Saint John's Methodist Church, the choice of Beverly and her parents. They weren't a really religious family, but they were members of this church and since they were paying for the wedding, it didn't matter to me. I had been raised a Catholic and according to the guidelines of my religion, if we weren't married in the Catholic Church, it didn't really count. That would take on a ridiculous logic in my thinking down the road.

The service was short by Catholic standards, and after a brief reception, we were off to Williamsburg, Virginia, for our honeymoon. I had only taken a few days of leave, so it was going to be a (short) long weekend honeymoon. In spite of that, I was extremely excited and eager to carry her over the threshold of the hotel. To her credit, Beverly had maintained her virginity despite my best advances, and I was ready to culminate the total romantic part of our relationship.

The honeymoon was not quite what I had expected, at no fault of Beverly's. It was primarily because I started drinking at the reception and was almost drunk before we got to the hotel. I remember going to get ice outside the door before we were to head into an indescribable state of ecstasy because I feared I might pass out before the big moment. We somehow managed to get through it, but I don't believe either of us felt like we had culminated anything. In fact, I don't believe romance was ever a top priority in Beverly's life, except for the romantic occasions when we wanted to try to have children. I'm also quite sure my excessive drinking was a turn-off, even at the times when romance may have been in the air. For my part, I was always basically trying to fulfill my lust drive, which was often fueled by alcohol. Drinking was starting to be a problem, but I couldn't see it. That would change.

Hitchhiking home on Friday nights continued, but since we were married we would stay with Beverly's grandmother, Nanny, from Friday until Sunday night. Nanny was the family matriarch and probably the coolest old Southern woman I ever met—and surely the best cook.

She lived with Granddaddy in a small two-bedroom house in a modest part of Norfolk. Granddaddy was a retired barber, and I think that every time I saw him he had an Al Capone–type of hat on. Inside or outside, he always had the hat on. He had been a bit reckless in his youth. In fact, as the story goes, he had abandoned the family for a few years and came back after "wasting his substance on unrighteous living." He was allowed back on the condition that he would never speak of it and treat Nanny like the queen she was. These were some of the secrets he shared with me in our few moments alone. He must have felt we had something in common.

Beverly and I continued our dreaming about the big house we would have someday as we drove around endlessly in our 1960 Chevrolet looking at neighborhoods. Being realistic, we knew we were going to have to live in an apartment for a while, but we could dream.

In February of 1966, I got orders to my first choice of duty stations and was sent to the marine barracks at the Naval Station Norfolk. I would be close to home, Beverly and I would get our own place, and life would be grand.

Because of my security clearance, I was doing guard duty and sentry duty for the Armed Forces Staff College in Norfolk, a war college where senior-grade officers from all of the NATO countries learn tactics and strategies in times of war. I did this until my promotion to corporal in July of 1966, at which time I became corporal of the guard. With that promotion, I supervised the sentries who were guarding the base. It is considered plush duty as long as the sentries stay awake and don't play quick draw with their loaded .45 caliber pistols. We were already starting to get some returning Vietnam vets, and they were a little more unstable on average than the marines who hadn't been there yet.

We did have a quick-draw incident in which a sentry was killed, as well as a suicide prior to my arrival, so I was watching things very closely. I am pleased to say that we had no incidents to report on my watch—oh yeah, except for the sentry who pulled his pistol out and threatened to shoot a Navy ensign's wife's dog. As the story was passed on to me, it went like this: he had stopped her to ask to see her ID card, which all military personnel and their dependents get. Depending on the security level, it is sometimes required to get on base. She was insulted because she wasn't just waved through and saluted by virtue of her officer's decal. It works that way sometimes, but not this time. It is conceivable the sentry just wanted to talk to her because she was attractive, but she wasn't interested in developing a relationship. She just wanted to get on the base. As the sentry reached through the driver's window to get the ID card, her dog came from the back seat and took a snap at his hand. Whether he was not thinking or just showing off, he pulled out his pistol and told the woman that he ought to just shoot her dog. He then gave her back her ID and waved her through. Understandably, we got a call, and he got sent away. The Vietnam War was starting to show itself in strange ways.

Beverly and I had gotten ourselves a little apartment not far from the naval base. It became apparent right away that I had married a woman who had high standards of living. It seemed our dreams were now in a position to come true. But she was greatly influenced by her well-to-do relatives in Newbern, North Carolina, and I still had that desire to look good. It was a bad combination for nineteen-year-old newlyweds.

My corporal's pay and her income from her job weren't enough to allow us to live quite as worldly as we wanted, but there was available credit. She had gotten a scholarship in high school to a beauty school, and upon her completion she worked endlessly to try to keep us looking good. She also kept that little apartment so clean that it was like living in a model home twenty-four hours a day.

After painting the place and buying all the Ethan Allen furniture and rugs we could get on credit, we were indeed looking good. Unfortunately, this coincided with my starting to stop off at the local bar on the way home and spending money that was supposed to help pay for all these nice things. In fact, it became a regular habit of mine to tell her that I would be home for dinner at six but rarely make it before nine. Somehow I had convinced myself that if she would make things better at home, I would want to come home. The reality is that I wanted to stay out and drink. This started causing major problems in the relationship. She wanted this stereotypical lovely home and I did too, but once I drank that first beer, my brain would go into tilt mode. Shooting pool and talking about the world's problems became more attractive to me than going home, and yet there was a part of me that wanted that lovely home as well. It all became very confusing for both of us. The idea that I might have a drinking problem never crossed my mind. The poor girl was trying her best, but it could never be enough. Things were about to change.

chapter 11

The Greatest Job in the Marine Corps

In July of 1966, I got called into the sergeant major's office, and
he told me that I had been selected to be the admiral's driver.
I'm sure it was based on my having a security clearance; in fact,
in order to be a flag officer's (admiral's or general's) driver, he said
top secret clearance was necessary. In short order I was promoted
to sergeant and given top secret security clearance. I felt like I had
arrived as far as my career was concerned. I was on the fast track.
Now if I could just get Beverly to want me to come home and rec-
ognize how important I was, I figured, everything would be great.
My partying continued to be a problem. There was a part of me
that wanted to stay home, but another part of me wanted to get
away and prove my "manhood" in combat. The admiral would be
able to help me with that.

It was warm that night, and I had just dropped the admiral
off at a fancy function that admirals sometimes have to go to.
Admiral Reynolds D. Hogle was a fine man, and as commandant
of the 5th Naval District, he was apparently good at what he did.
Furthermore, driving for a Navy admiral had to be the greatest
job in the marines. Along with my security clearance, I wore

dress blues and drove a big, black staff car with flags flying from the fenders, stars on the license plates, and the lights on. Damn, I looked cool. In the office, we always had an abundance of good-looking Navy women, called WAVES, working the admin duties while trying to ignore the flirtatious advances made by the men around them. (This was well before the military discovered that women could do almost all of the duties the men could do and oftentimes do them better.) It was a dream job for a young marine.

You would think a guy would relish this duty, especially when you consider that whenever I dropped off the admiral for an evening social event, I usually stopped off at one of the bars and drank beer and shot pool until it was time to pick him up. I would park that big, black staff car with the flags flying and stars blazing out in front of the place and raise the eyebrows of the Shore Patrol, the Navy's military police, who were, I'm sure, wondering what the admiral might be doing in Bunny's Tradewinds Bar and Grill. I never got asked. It was obvious that drinking had become part of my decision-making formula. I felt that my being able to have a few beers was in the realm of sound reasoning. Admirals' staff cars never got pulled over, even when the driver seemed to be a little drunk. I mean, it could all be part of a top secret mission.

In spite of all of this freedom, I didn't feel that driving for an admiral was really being a marine. That chance would soon come.

By the middle of 1966, the marines had started getting more seriously involved in the Vietnam War. While driving the admiral back from one of the socials and fueled with a couple of brews, I looked in the rearview mirror and said, "With all due respect, sir, I think I want to get involved in that war before it's over." He, being a wise old sage, asked, "Now, sergeant, are you sure you want to get involved in that mess?" Jokingly, I replied," Well, sir, I *am* a trained killer." We both laughed, and he said, "Well, I'm sure we can get you over there." They did too. Admirals don't want anyone driving for them who doesn't want to be driving for them.

chapter 12

1967: The Combat Days

It wasn't long before I was on my way to California for some guerrilla warfare training and then on to prove I was a real marine. Since I had been promoted to sergeant prior to arriving in Okinawa, I was going to be a squad leader. A marine rifle squad is made up of twelve marines and a squad leader. The bonds get close very quickly because unless you learn to work together, the life expectancy is very short once you get into combat.

In May of 1967, our resupplied and re-outfitted battalion, the Third Battalion 4th Marines, nicknamed "The Thundering Third," flew out of Okinawa after about sixty days of jungle training, on a C-130 cargo-type plane.

We arrived in Dong Ha at about midnight. I was the third squad leader of the 3rd Platoon, Mike Company. We had lost a lot of marines over the previous few months performing operations around the Quang Tri Province . Dong Ha was a base camp north of Da Nang and close to the demilitarized zone (DMZ), the line that separates North and South Vietnam. Those C-130s apparently have no heat, and as we got up to our cruising altitude, we started freezing our asses off. The flight took about four hours, and when we landed, we went from freezing to what seemed like 105 degrees and 100 percent humidity. Ugh! As we came down the ramp, the heat literally took our breath away. It wasn't an hour later, as we were digging in, that the gooks, one of the many names we a used referring to the Vietcong or North Vietnamese Army, started the rocket and mortar attacks. I mean, give us a break! Can't we at least get a little hunkering down time? I guess not. It seems the gooks already had the holes we were digging targeted, and they didn't waste any time welcoming us to our new home. I think we had two marines killed that night. We also had a chance to see Doc Jones, one of our platoon's Navy corpsmen, in action. He was all over the place assisting everyone who needed it and responding to each call of "Corpsman up" with total disregard for his own safety. I believe he got a decoration the first night we were in country.

Within just a couple of days, we were humping out to our landing zone to board choppers for our first operation. It would be one to remember. Operation Hickory was going to take us all the way up toward the DMZ. It seems the North Vietnamese Army (NVA) had one of their toughest regiments gathering for their own incursion en masse toward the south and was going to turn what was a guerrilla war into a full-scale major assault.

Our job was to get to them before they got to us. Even though our outfit was made up of a bunch of green peas (new guys) whom we had picked up in Okinawa, including me, we were anxious to "get into the shit." The landing zone was expected to be hot so we didn't quite know what to expect, but we knew what we were supposed to do when we landed—get the hell off the chopper and set up a perimeter for the remaining choppers to land. Fortunately, the landing zone was quiet and we were soon heading out to complete our first objective—find the NVA.

After a few days of searching, we were getting a little discouraged and thought perhaps we had missed our chance for contact. It seemed like all we were doing was walking, sweating, and bitching. On about day four of the operation, we started moving toward a small jungle mountain range that had been bombed extensively when the NVA were first spotted days before. It was difficult enough just to get up that mountain on the first day. The pass was only wide enough for a single file and perfect for an enemy ambush. The NVA were sitting in a bunker across a deep ravine about seventy-five yards away.

First squad led the way, and as soon as the first four-man fire team crossed over the bomb crater that had been made a few days earlier, things erupted. Machine gun and small-arms fire opened up on the rest of the squad from the enemy bunker, and we instantly lost three guys from the first squad. The rest of us were wondering what the hell was going on and felt helpless to take action because of the narrowness of the trail. All we heard was yelling and hollering and gunfire. First squad was pinned down in the crater, and the fire was so intense that they couldn't move.

As soon as we got word of what had happened, we headed back up the hill to get the boys out of the crater and try to silence the machine gun. The chaos was maddening, and the challenge was to try to take out the bunker while minimizing casualties. We did manage to direct our fire at the bunker long enough to get the men out of the crater, but we could not get to the three dead marines. They had been the lead fire team and had crossed through the crater when they got blasted. We had to leave them to drop back and regroup—to decide which squad was going to take point, go back, and retrieve the bodies. In the Corps, we don't leave our dead, even if it means more fucking dead to get them.

Second squad drew the point on day two, and as they were cautiously inching their way up the side of that jungle slope, once again the shit hit the fan. As soon as the first fire team reached the crater, the enemy machine guns in the bunker opened fire, pinning them down.

But this time we had a little more warning and quickly returned fire. After returning considerable fire at the bunker and obliterating the surrounding jungle terrain, they were able to come back down the hill—still, however, without the dead marines.

Because of the thickness of the jungle, it was impossible to get any successful air support, and it was obvious that the only way to get these marines' bodies was to go back up and get them. As the third squad leader, I knew that my squad was next to go up that mountain, so at the meeting that night to review the third day's plan with the platoon sergeant and our first lieutenant, I thought I needed to offer my recommendations as to how we should approach things a little differently since we already knew what the first two days had brought. I was quickly rebuffed and told just to get my ass up there and get those bodies. All I really wanted to do was suggest we put a couple of guys down on the left flank or perhaps send a team to the other side of the ravine to obliterate the bunker and any other bunkers from that side. It seemed reasonable to me, especially since it was going to be my squad going up that hill. But as they say, ours is not to reason why; ours is just to do or die. So, come on, guys. Let's go fucking die.

I met with my team leaders that night and told them I wanted to send out a couple of flank guys to watch that bunker as we made our journey up the hill. I didn't ask; I just did it. It was my first case of deciding it was better to ask for forgiveness than to ask permission from people who weren't aware of what was going on. There would be many more. I also told all the guys to say whatever prayers they felt would work for them and get right with their God.

On day three, we headed up that hill. I'm not sure if it was the flank guys or the prayers, but we got up that hill without a shot being fired. That's the good news. The bad news is that picking up three of your fellow marines who have been lying in the 105 degree sun for three days while you're waiting to get your ass shot off is not the way to start your day. The idea is to slip ponchos underneath their bodies without causing their skin or even limbs to fall off and to try to do it all with as much dignity as possible. The stench is horrible, and flies and maggots are everywhere. But third squad got those marines off of that fucking hill. I told my guys how proud I was of them and that even though that type of mission isn't deserving of a medal, it's certainly deserving of a little R&R. But that wouldn't come for a while. I kept thinking, *I requested this?*

chapter 13

Frank Hardy: The Unlikely Hero

After a day or two of laying low, except for sending out nightly ambushes, we headed off in a new direction. We started cautiously moving up a thicker group of jungle hills, still looking for that NVA regiment. The plan was to catch the NVA as they were withdrawing from extensive shelling. We would be going into areas right on the Ben Hai River and searching villages with locals who had never even seen Americans. The rumor was that the people in these villages had been loyal to the NVA and had stored caches of rice and weapons to be used in their incursions south. As we moved up this one extremely thick jungle hill, we started drawing heavy fire from across a ravine to our left. We immediately responded with devastating machine gun fire, but to no avail.

The NVA were deeply entrenched, and whenever we blasted them they went underground until the firing let up. Then would open up on us from a different location, perhaps thirty yards to the right or left. One of our platoon leaders toward the rear decided to blast them with CS gas grenades, a type of tear gas that usually makes people come out in the open or do a vanishing act. It wasn't a bad strategy, but from the rear no one considered the wind up in the front until it was too late. As the gas started rising, it came right back in third platoon's faces. As was the norm, we had left our gas masks about five hundred yards to the rear because of the thickness of the jungle. We were now sitting ducks to be victims of our own gas attack.

I called back to the rear to ask if the right upper flank had been cleared and checked out. We had to get to higher ground and perhaps get over the ridge to avoid the gas. I was reassured that it had, so we started dragging our asses up the hill to regroup and clear our heads and eyes. After hacking our way up the hill, our point man, Frank Hardy, and I were leading the way. We usually moved patiently through such thick jungle, but time was of the essence considering the circumstances. As we all reached a point just below the crest of the hill and tried to catch our breath, Frank, in his most unique style of communicating, said, "Who was the dumb motherfucker ..." Those were his last words.

As he shoved me out of the way, his words made him the first target and sealed his fate. Gunfire erupted, and everyone hit the ground.

✱

The distinct AK-47 shots rang out—pop-pop-pop. Three shots caught Frank directly in the head. As I was frantically firing my M16 while trying to reach Frank, he seemed frozen and refused to drop. His head was already swelling up, and it was obvious he was dead before he hit the ground. Angrily moving to the hill crest, I opened fire in the direction of the AK and, before I could come to my senses, had blasted everything in front of us. One of our corpsman moved up to the hill crest and started working on Frank, but it was hopeless. As we searched the hill crest, the NVA had once again disappeared.

I'll never know if I got the gook who shot Frank. I can only hope. The way I saw it, Frank Hardy had died saving my life, and it would stay with me forever. As usual, he saw what we couldn't see and acted instinctively to save his squad leader. But it wasn't me—he would have done that for any one of his fellow marines. Chaos once again ruled, but this was different. Frank was my point man, and he was also my friend, a link to home. He was from Portsmouth, and I was from Norfolk, just two miles away. We knew the names of the same places, and even though we had never met before Vietnam, we had that special bond only brothers in combat can understand. *My God,* I thought, *how did I get in this crazy situation anyway? Oh, yeah. I volunteered.*

As we continued Operation Hickory, our outfit took on the standard look of most grunt outfits in Vietnam. We were looking for the enemy and trying to do it without being spotted. Since we had lost a few guys, we were shorthanded as we were cutting through the jungle on our way to a village that sat right on the Ben Hai River.

The Ben Hai is the river that separates North and South Vietnam. My navigation guy and I took the point since Frank was gone and the radioman was right behind me. The jungle was extremely thick, and the elephant grass was doing a job slicing our hands and arms as we worked the machetes and bayonets to cut through toward the village, unseen. When we finally broke through, we came upon a village full of surprised Vietnamese. They had never seen Americans and surely had been told by the NVA that we would kill them all when we got there. They were scared to death.

Typically, we would look for an overabundance of rice and other items that would indicate a village loyal to the NVA. We found that and more. We discovered weapons and ammunition that wouldn't normally be held in a village. Of course, the villagers denied knowing anything, indicating that the gooks had these folks too scared to say anything. They had a habit of killing anyone who talked and sometimes would kill a village chief just to prove a point.

These poor villagers were in a very awkward position. I felt sad for them. We started rounding them all up to relocate them by chopper to start life over. As we were searching every possible hiding place for gooks, it was obvious there was someone in one of the bunkers.

After trying to talk them out by way of our broken Vietnamese, I had one of my team leaders toss a few grenades and finally a white phosphorus grenade in to try to flush them out, to no avail. We figured the grenades had probably killed anyone in there, but with tunnels and winding corners you never can be sure. I told Jimmy Doyle, my "tunnel rat," to go find out what was left in there. A marine tunnel rat is usually smaller than average and has balls as big as basketballs. Jimmy was no exception. Armed with a flashlight and a .45 caliber pistol, he headed in to see what was left to deal with. After about five minutes, we heard two shots fired and anxiously waited to see who would exit. Jimmy first tossed a dog out of the entrance and then dragged a dead woman out by her hair, the only way he could get her out. The reality of war was embedding itself deep in my psyche.

As we walked the villagers to the landing zone to send them off to be "saved," it dawned on me that these folks hadn't volunteered. What a shit sandwich they got served.

We started humping our way back to the next village following some of the previously carved-out trails, so it wasn't quite as difficult to make our way. After three nights of inactivity, it became apparent to me that my arms were swollen and covered with sores from the jungle hacking a few days earlier. The humidity and the inability for these small cuts to heal apparently had allowed them to become badly infected. I had been constantly brushing flies off of my arms as they would land, but they would come back instantly.

The infection and pain was so great that I had resorted to spitting at the flies to get them off. When it finally got to the point that I couldn't take off my flak jacket, I went to the corpsman and asked if he had any medicine to put on it. He took one look and stuck a thermometer in my mouth. He then immediately told me to sit down and said I was going to the hospital in Da Nang for treatment. He said I had a 104 degree temperature and, after giving me some kind of pills, said I would be on the next chopper out. He called it jungle rot. It was not a very glorious reason to be taken out of a combat zone, but I guess he knew the emergency nature of the infection. In six hours, I was in Da Nang.

chapter 14

God and Beer

As I lay on my bed with the IVs running into both arms full of some kind of penicillin, it dawned on me that I had lost my dog tags and my watch while cutting through that jungle. I could get new dog tags, but the watch had been a graduation gift from Mom and Dad and was sort of my connection to home. In combat, those mementos meant a great deal. The watch had my name on it and was covered with a dark green tape on a chain around my neck, along with my dog tags. This was standard practice to keep everything shiny from being seen by a potential enemy. I was bummed out.

After three or four days, I was starting to feel a bit better, and even though my arms and hands were still all wrapped up, I was down to one IV. The ward at the hospital consisted of Quonset huts with about twenty beds on each side and a passageway down the middle. We were constantly getting in new wounded each day; some were walking wounded, and some were stretchered in. On day four, a bandaged marine came down the center of the ward, and on the chain around his neck was my watch. I hollered out to him, "Hey, marine! You got my watch." He responded with a blank stare.

"You Gorman?" I said I was. He took off the chain and tossed me my watch and dog tags. *A miracle*, I thought. Apparently he had followed the trail we had chopped through the jungle and along the way found my belongings. Then he got shot and was sent to the same ward I was in. Strange things were starting to happen. They would get stranger.

The infection seemed to be a little tougher to kick than the Navy docs thought it would be, and I stayed in that hospital bed for about three weeks. They wanted to keep me close for another week or so after that, but I was able to leave the ward and go out on the base grounds. This meant I could go to the club, fill my gut with much-desired beer, and bullshit with some of the other grunts. I also decided to go reconnect with church since the impending return to my outfit meant I may end up getting my ass shot off. In fact, the hospital compound was getting rocketed and mortared by the gooks every few days, so survival was kind of questionable.

I went to mass every day and bargained with God: if he spared my life, I would be sure to continue going to mass and confession each week and probably do charity work and help the poor for the rest of my life. Then I would go to the club fully confident that I was destined for sainthood if I survived. *But, as for now*, I reasoned, *I'll just have "one more" beer.*

After thirty days of treatment, I jumped on a chopper and headed back to my outfit. The unit was back in Dong Ha awaiting our next operation, and within a few days we were boarding choppers and going back to the bush. Operation Cimarron was just like most operations—try to find the gooks and eliminate them. Along the way, we would usually set up camp, dig holes in anticipation of the common rocketing that sometimes took place, and send out ambushes.

On my third day back, it was my squad's night for an ambush. This would be my first ambush without Frank Hardy as my point man, and I was a little uneasy. We had a couple of brand new guys.

The usual routine was to leave the perimeter of the camp at dusk so we could recon (check out) the area while we still had daylight and then set up an ambush along a potential trail to catch the enemy going or coming from one position to another. Generally, since we were already on the NVA doorstep, a squad ambush this far north would go out only about one or two klicks away, maybe two miles at best.

On this particular night, on the way out, we walked right through an enemy base camp that had been freshly vacated. This indicated that they would probably be returning late in the evening, after they had done their rocketing or mortaring for the night. That was their routine. In other words, it seemed a sure thing that we would have contact that night, so we were very cautious in setting up our "bush." The strategy was to find a likely return path for the gooks and place the squad in an L shape facing out so that we wouldn't be shooting each other if we encountered contact. Two teams would be on the long line of the L and one team on the short end. The squad leader and radioman were usually positioned at the bend of the L to control things easily. Since silence was important, especially at night, there would be a tie line cord connecting each individual; then, if anyone saw something, he would jerk on it to alarm the rest of us before opening fire.

Everything was quiet for the first few hours, although it was one of those pitch black nights with no moon and no wind. It was a typical spooky Vietnam jungle night. As we sat and looked into that black jungle, it wasn't long before everything started looking like a gook with an AK-47 trained right on us, so fire control was very important. At about two in the morning, without a moment's notice, the team on the far right opened fire, scaring the shit out of everybody—no jerking of the cord, no warning, no nothing. Within seconds, the entire ambush opened fire and all hell broke loose. After realizing that there was no return fire, I yelled for a cease fire and scrambled the few feet to the first team to find out what the fuck was going on. Their response was, "I saw something move, Sarge."

I told everyone to sit tight and not move. Within a minute from the first shots, the radio started blaring, "Mike three 3, Mike three 3. This is Mike Actual. What the hell's going on out there? Over." Mike Actual referred to the skipper of Mike company, and Mike three 3 was the third platoon, third squad—us.

A radio blaring in the still of the night, particularly after the world has just exploded and suddenly become silent, seems as loud as the PA system at Yankee Stadium. Since we had just given our position away, I didn't respond. I wasn't going to go from ambusher to ambushee. But the captain was very persistent and kept blaring. My nervous radioman kept handing me the mouthpiece until, much to everyone's surprise, I told him to turn the damn thing off.

"The book" called for us to change position once we had given it away. Sometimes the book is wrong, and this was one of those times. With a known enemy camp behind us and an unknown whatever in front of us, I talked the situation over with my team leaders and we decided to just stay put. It's a good thing too. My fucking ears were ringing so loud I thought my head would explode.

As was usually the case, I knew the skipper would want a body count. At dawn we were to head back to our base camp and, based on our findings, I figured we had opened up on a "squad of baboons." Shaking my head and even chuckling a bit, I told my radioman to turn the radio back on, and we cautiously headed in.

I was extremely dizzy as we went back and wondered if in fact my eardrums were gone. Once we returned, I explained the situation to the skipper, and he seemed to concur that I had done the right thing. I still got the feeling he wanted a body count, but I had nothing for him.

It wasn't long before the ear problem worsened, and the diagnosis was inner ear damage. That's where the dizziness came from. I was sent to the hospital ship *USS Repose* for extensive testing. As it turned out, I had reinjured my eardrums, and before long I was on my way to the Naval Medical Center in Portsmouth, Virginia, by way of Yokosuka, Japan.

chapter 15

Home from the War

e flew into Andrews Air Force Base in Maryland on a big C-141 medical evacuation jet, and from there I was transferred to Naval Medical Center in Virginia. I would continue to be tested at Portsmouth and treated as a convalescent patient until my ears healed and my equilibrium got back to normal. The ringing and headaches that sporadically accompanied it never went away, but my hearing, according to the doctors, was within acceptable limits. As a convalescent, I could leave during the day but had to be back by 6:00 a.m. when the doctors made their rounds.

Since my return was unexpected, after Beverly made a few visits to the hospital, she went ahead and attended her preplanned family reunion in Hazlehurst, Georgia. It was an annual event for her family, and I encouraged her to go ahead and go. I was going to be laid up for a while, and we would be able to see plenty of each other now that I was home. The reality was that I could already taste the cold beer waiting for me, and I wanted a few unencumbered nights on the town before I settled in to being a husband. Beverly had bought us a new '67 Mustang and left the keys at the hospital before she left. With all of this new freedom, the drinking was about to take off with a vengeance.

I spent my first night on the town in uniform, trying to gain all the glory I could as a returning combat veteran marine sergeant. I had invited a buddy of mine to go out drinking with me in my new car, and after getting completely smashed, it was time to head back to the hospital. I stopped to get gas at about two in the morning, and as I pulled away from the pump, I suddenly stopped and asked my buddy if he wanted to get a late bite to eat. Of course he said yes, so, trying to be cool, I slammed the car into reverse and floored it. Fortunately, the attendant who had pumped the gas was away from the island because I wiped out both pumps and demolished the rear end of the fragile little Mustang. My friend and I stumbled out of the car and surveyed the damage before the police got there. We already had our story made up about having to get back to the hospital for treatment for the severe war wounds we had suffered in "the Nam."

Thank God for an understanding cop; he helped us get a cab and tow truck and reassured us that insurance would take care of everything, including the gas pumps. Hmm, now who was going to take care of explaining this to Beverly?

After a few weeks in the hospital, I was transferred to the marine barracks at the Portsmouth Naval Shipyard, where I would be the sergeant of the guard. This meant I would drive around in a pickup truck with a red light on top of it and drop off the gate guards as well as keep an eye on the overall perimeter of that base. I carried a loaded .45 caliber pistol and wore the standard uniform of the day. It was really easy duty considering where I had come from, and it allowed me a lot of free time to drink at the enlisted club or one of the many bars just outside the main gate. In fact, I had become so emboldened by this new freedom that I sometimes drove the truck around the base while on duty with a fourteen-ounce can of beer in my lap. A loaded .45 and a fourteen-ounce beer are not really a good combination, but somehow I justified it, thinking I was in control.

Beverly and I had gotten a small two-bedroom home at the

military housing complex available to married noncommissioned officers. Even though it was a very modest, clapboard house left over from WWII, Beverly immediately turned it into the cleanest, most well-decorated and -furnished place in the entire neighborhood, as was her style. She was unbelievable, making it a gorgeous place that any loving husband would want to come home to.

I was a loving husband, but I couldn't seem to make it home until I was pretty well plastered.

Somehow I reasoned once again that if she *made* me want to come home, I would. The thought that I needed to stop drinking never crossed my mind. The routine became standard. I would come home drunk, she would start yelling and crying, and I would leave to go get drunker. I would then come home to a silent house and make promises that I would change: "From now on, things will be different." I was sincere too. But once I started on that next beer, my thinking changed.

After months of this on-again, off-again disappointment, we surmised that maybe the problem was that we had never gotten married in a Catholic church. So off we went to the Holy Angels Catholic Church for instructions and then had our marriage blessed in the church. This kept us hopeful for a short period of time, but it was to no avail. Once I took that first drink, all bets were off. I had come to the conclusion that the real problem was that I had gotten married too young and hadn't had time to sow my wild oats. "Yeah, that's what it was," I told myself. Since I wasn't coming home anyway, we decided to separate.

I also believed that I needed to drink to forget the events of Vietnam and accept this constant pain-in-the-ass ringing in my ears. I didn't pay much attention to it when I was living the partying, drunken marine role. There wasn't much talk about post-traumatic stress disorder in those days. I guess alcohol was serving a medicinal purpose for me. The dosage was soon to go up and cause more problems than ringing ears.

chapter 16

1968: Panic Attacks and the Psych Ward

When Beverly and I split, I moved into the barracks, and she got the ball rolling on a divorce. Now I was free to do whatever I wanted—of course, this meant drinking with the boys and trying to figure this whole *life* thing out. Part of me loved Beverly and was saddened that I had put her through such hell, but another part of me knew I couldn't stop the drinking. I knew I had to stop the memories and the damn ringing.

One night as I was drinking with a buddy in the base club called Tun's Tavern, named after the famous bar where the first US Marines had been recruited on November 10, 1775, I was overwhelmed by a feeling of shortness of breath and tightness in my chest.

For some unexplained reason, I felt like I was going to die. I told my buddy that he needed to take me to the emergency room because I thought I might be having a heart attack. He freaked out a bit and whisked me away in his Pontiac GTO, heading to the hospital about three miles away. As we walked in, a Navy corpsman checked my vital signs, told me to have a seat, and said he would have the doctor check me out. The doctor had some

X-rays and tests run, and when he returned, he said all of them looked okay and sent me on my way. I felt somewhat relieved, but not much. It was the first time in my life, other than when I was sitting on that ambush that I felt out of control. There would be many more.

Panic attacks and various phobias started taking over my life. I had started avoiding any situation from which I couldn't immediately escape. This included driving on bridges, riding in elevators, and flying on planes, and it even got to a point that I wouldn't drive on freeways because I felt I could be trapped in between exits. I could avoid most of these situations, but the panic attacks were inescapable.

Whenever I was alone, the dreaded tightness in my chest and shortness of breath returned, always followed by the fear of suddenly dying. I would struggle through the days' work until I was free to drink. Then I would try to avoid the panic through barroom activities, such as shooting pool and talking trash, always dreading closing time. After the bars closed, I couldn't go back to the barracks for fear of the panic returning, so I would drive around all night drinking beer and staying close to the ER of the naval hospital.

I had checked in a couple of more times and each time was told there was nothing wrong with me physically. I walked out of the ER each time, starting to doubt the doctor's capabilities. I was convinced they had missed something and that there was something terribly wrong with me. There was; I just didn't know what it was, and apparently neither did they. I was starting to do some self-diagnosis and believed it must be related to Vietnam or my wife or my alcoholic mother or the Catholic church or whatever. *It's a good thing there's cold beer available or I would really be in trouble*, I thought.

Within a few months, as I was sitting in my car behind the hospital one night, I was approached by a Navy corpsman. He had probably seen me before, but this time he recommended I come inside. I was soon admitted to the psychiatric ward for a more in-depth look at what was going on with me. It was 1968, and wounded marines and sailors were everywhere in the hospital. I surmised that my panic issues were not on top of the priority list for the medical staff, but the Navy shrinks were trying to help me the best that they could. After a week of being in a confined environment, I seemed to be doing a little better, and because I was a sergeant and doing so well, they made me the master at arms of the psych ward. I thought, *Back on top again, even in the nut ward.* It never dawned on me or the doctors that a week in a controlled environment was just the amount of time it took for me to detox.

As was usual, when you're making good progress, you are allowed to go out on liberty in the afternoon as long as you are back for the doctors' rounds in the early morning. I was familiar with that practice from my earlier ear problem hospitalization, and my pattern on liberty stayed the same. Before long, I was at the George Washington Bar and Grill, and this time when the joint closed, I had a safe place to go. The psych ward seemed like an oasis.

As the master at arms, my job was to wake up all of the other patients. It's a difficult task in a "nut ward" because nuts don't respond well to discipline. Whenever I would say, "Get up! It's time to serve Uncle Sam," they would often just scowl and roll over. I mean, the thinking seemed to be, *What are you going to do—lock me up in a nut ward?*

Being a marine sergeant, I wasn't used to being ignored when I gave an order, especially when I had been out drunk till two o'clock the night before. I endured the "responsibility without authority" frustration for as long as I could, until this one particular day. It was time to rise and shine, and when I said, "Get up," this one fellow who had been a constant thorn in my side didn't move, so

I just dumped his bed over and rolled him out on the floor. This caused quite a stir on the ward, and I was promptly put in an isolation room so the staff could find out what all my anger was about.

After a few days of one-on-one with the shrink, talking about Mom and Dad, Beverly, churches, and Vietnam ad nauseam, I was diagnosed with a passive aggressive personality.

The doctor finally asked me if I wanted to take an honorable discharge as a result of my medical condition. I remember the conversation very clearly. I told him that I wanted to live without sitting in my car behind the hospital "waiting to die" and asked him for his recommendation. He told me that the panic would probably go away once I was away from the regimentation of the military. I reminded him that I had been on active duty for almost four years and had even extended my service when it was possible, so that didn't make a lot of sense to me. He then suggested that the disorder sometimes shows up at different times with different people. With this little ray of hope, I took the discharge and left my beloved Marine Corps. I was sad but hopeful. Drinking was never discussed throughout the entire process. I probably would have lied about how much I drank anyway. In fact, I believed that without drinking, I would really be screwed up. It was April of 1968, and I was twenty-one years old—way too young to be an alcoholic.

chapter 17

My Dad's LARS Theory

A rmed with this new enthusiasm for life, I decided that it was time to start on a new career. My dad had retired from the Navy and had started selling life insurance. He had been reasonably successful and was one of the few people I trusted at this stage of my life for guidance. He suggested that I look into sales since I had done so much selling as a kid and outgoing personalities are sometimes an advantage. I took his advice, and before long I was selling life insurance for the Prudential Insurance Company of America.

I had started talking to Beverly when I knew I was getting out of the Corps and renewed her hope about rekindling our relationship. By that time she had taken the necessary action to get us divorced. Since I was a Catholic and knew they didn't believe in divorce, I didn't consider us really divorced. My theory was based on what I had learned from the Catholic church about divorce, which seemed to suggest that you could divorce but could never have sex again. If you did, you would be in "sin" and need to go to confession, which you can't do if you're divorced. Hmm, doomed to eternal damnation at twenty-one? Being a young man with a reasonable libido, that didn't seem like something I could go along with.

Since we both agreed that I was certainly going to become a highly successful insurance executive, we got back together and went to the justice of the peace to remarry. After all, we were married in the eyes of Catholic church by then. God would certainly like that. I guess if you drink enough beer, you can convince yourself of anything. I thought I would talk everything over with my dad.

My dad was a man of uncanny logic and taught me many things, most of which became more important as I got older. He had a philosophy that would resonate with me all of my life. He said he got it from a Navy chaplain as he prepared to leave the Navy. It was the LARS theory. The theory suggests that to be well rounded, all people have the need for four basic things in life: 1) love, 2) adventure, 3) recognition, and 4) security. He suggested that as I went through life, I should ask if any of those four are lacking and then do what I can to fill the void.

✱

To take care of the security and recognition parts of Dad's theory, I felt like selling insurance would be the way to go. Once I got the necessary licenses and passed the company tests, I was off and running. He also suggested I go talk to the most successful salesman in the company to see what they are doing and then duplicate it.

As is usually the case, successful people are always happy to share their ideas as long as you aren't going to be competing in their territory. Cal Tatum was the top producer in the office and was one of these guys.

My territory was in a young adult, highly transient, military part of Norfolk, Virginia. Cal taught me to ride up and down the neighborhood streets and write down the locations of all of the empty apartments. Then the next week, I would do the same and see which apartments were no longer empty. That meant someone had just moved in. It was important to get to those people quickly, before they had been harassed by every insurance, vacuum cleaner, and pot-and-pan salesman in town. When they were new "move-ins," they were friendly and generally more open to talk to strangers.

It's safe to say that in the first ninety days of my new job, I sold more insurance than anyone else in the office. In fact, I seemed to be able to shine and excel at everything I did for about ninety days. This "career" would be no different. Oh, yeah, I was back on top again. It certainly was deserving of celebration. Newly committed to my marriage, high-flying insurance superstar on the rise—yep, it's time for a couple of cold beers before going home to my loving wife.

Beverly and I had gotten a relatively nice apartment in the heart of Norfolk near my territory and, of course, near a few hot night-spots. The struggles started soon after we moved in. Once again, Beverly created a beautiful home and, after getting some of our Ethan Allen furniture back from relatives, the place was decked out. She was giving it her best shot. But as usual, once the party began, all of my values went out the window. Before long, I couldn't ever get home without being half drunk, and my illustrious career at Prudential was starting to slide. Romance was not a big part of our life, but on one evening, being temporarily sober and following one of my promises to change, we made love and the stars must have been lined up right because our lovemaking culminated in a beautiful little girl.

Amy was born October 16, 1968, and the thing I noticed instantly was her big, brown eyes. I've always called her my brown-eyed angel. She was gorgeous. I told myself, "I've got to make a change for her sake if nothing else." But then there was the Lido Inn and the Green Wheel Inn. I had to go past them to get home. I couldn't make it home.

chapter 18

December 1968: Escaping into the Mental Hospital

B efore long, I quit the job at Prudential. My production was starting to suffer, and it was just a matter of time before there would be no production. The guilt was unbearable, and the panic attacks returned with a vengeance. I sought further psychiatric help because I was now sitting in my car behind the Norfolk General Hospital emergency room waiting to die.

The doctors admitted me to the psych ward. I was hopeful the civilian doctors could figure this thing out. The first night I was there, I sneaked down on the locked elevator when visitors were leaving. Trying to look like a departing visitor, I wore a trench coat I had gotten from somewhere because it helped conceal the wristband and blue pajamas. The paper slippers would have been a dead giveaway, but fortunately the orderly didn't look at my feet. I didn't know what was going on, but I knew I needed a beer.

About a half a block from the hospital ER was the Philly Lounge. I had no idea it was a gay bar, not that it would have mattered, but it created an interesting situation. I kept my trench coat buttoned up to the neck, ordered a beer, and stated shooting pool. This beautiful blonde came up to the table and asked if she could shoot a game with me, and of course I said yes. Hmm, things were looking up. As the game went on, the blonde became a bit flirtatious, and to keep it alive I responded with my usual beer-induced "cool guy" personality. Suddenly, this short, stocky, fullback-looking woman came up to the pool table; told the blonde to have a seat; and told me that if I kept trying to pick up her woman, she was going to kick my ass. I responded that I wasn't trying to pick her up but, to save my manhood, I unbuttoned my trench coat, exposing my pajamas and wristband. I suggested that she might not want to try to kick my ass because I was already in the mental ward and couldn't guarantee my stability. Looking a bit surprised, she walked back to the blonde, shaking her head. I finished off a couple of more beers until I was out of money.

I guess a lot of people try to escape from mental wards, but I think I'm one of the few who had to figure out a way to get back into one. Walking back to the hospital and trying to put on my best dazed look, I told the ER staff that I had somehow ended up downstairs from the psych ward and didn't know how I got there. I had learned that mental patients can get away with just about anything. No one questioned me; they just took me back upstairs.

This was my first trip to a civilian mental ward, and I was optimistic. A few of the patients were undergoing shock treatment therapy, and after talking to some of them, I found that it erased certain memories, at least for a while. I was somewhat interested but didn't want to walk around looking weird for the few days after the treatment. Vanity is a terrible thing, plus the idea of being strapped down and losing total control had me a bit freaked out.

After a few days, my new psychiatrist, Dr. Thrasher, finally arrived on the scene. I don't even remember what we talked about for the ten minutes we spent together. I do remember that he never looked me in the eye; all he did was jot a few notes down on a clipboard. It seemed strange to me, but it would get stranger. After about a week of art therapy with crayons and pottery, administered by a variety of well-meaning social workers, I was discharged. I was then given an appointment with the good Dr. Thrasher for 9:30 p.m. a week later. I didn't understand the logic of such a late appointment, but I figured he must just be terribly busy, which meant he must be a great shrink. The reality was I could never get to 9:30 p.m. without being half drunk. It was never proven, but my theory today is that he was trying to see if I could get there sober. I couldn't.

After about two or three more late-night appointments, I surmised he was just too damn busy for me, and I never went back. We never discussed drinking. I probably would have lied anyway.

chapter *19*

Maybe I Can Sell Cars Drunk

B y early 1969, it was obvious to everyone in my family that I was in trouble emotionally and unable to take care of my young family. My dad and mom offered to let us move into the den of their home until I could get straightened out. I started looking in the newspaper for a job and came across an ad for a car salesman at Tidewater Dodge, just around the corner from where we lived. I figured that if I could sell insurance, an intangible product, then I ought to be able to sell a tangible product. I was right—before long I was selling Dodges and quite a few of them.

It was the days of the "muscle cars"—Chargers, Plymouth Roadrunners, and Dart Swingers—many with huge magnum multicarburetor engines and spoilers on the back. Man, they were cool, and of course, so was I. Within a couple of months, Beverly, Amy, and I moved into our own little apartment in Pinewood Gardens, a somewhat upscale, young adult neighborhood.

My first general sales manager was a short, little Italian guy named Dominic Lubertazzi. He stood about five-feet, four inches tall and wore silk suits, pointed-toed platform shoes, and shirts with ruffles at the sleeves. That was the style of the day. He always talked about how much money he made. "Do you know anybody else who makes thirty-five thousand dollars a year?" he would ask. *Wow*, I thought, *that's a ton of money*. I could see myself doing that. I was already showing signs of being good at this car-selling stuff. Surely it was just a matter of time. My used car manager, Larry Butkus, took me under his wing and tried to make me his protégé. According to some of the guys, he was the cousin of Dick Butkus, the great Chicago Bears football player, and he was just about as big.

His big mistake was taking me to lunch with him one afternoon and buying me a couple of beers to talk over this success journey. We ate at this Mexican restaurant called El Toro. They were well known for their hot sauce and chips. When you eat so much hot sauce, you have to drink a lot of beer, and we managed to keep the reputation intact. Before long, I was so drunk I could barely make it back to the dealership. I'm sure the bullshit was flowing freely, and Larry was convinced from then on that I drank a lot because of my Vietnam experience. I rode that excuse for all it was worth.

In spite of my new success, it wasn't long before I was looking for excuses as to why I couldn't stay consistent. Just as I had blamed Beverly for my not wanting to come home, I started blaming things at the dealership for my not wanting to work there anymore. The inventory was bad, managers were bad, there was no advertising, blah, blah. So I quit. Any dealership would want a sharp young guy like me, I figured. And many of them did—for a while anyway. I would always start off with a bang and raise the hopes of each new management staff, and then, after I found the nearest bar, I would blow it all. Sometimes I would disappear with the company cars for days at a time and often just call them to tell them where to pick it up, fearful of going back to face the music. I would usually burn all the bridges before I left.

Any money I made was drunk away, and in spite of her best

efforts, there was no way Beverly could pay the bills. She was handling the checkbook, and often I would sneak into the check box and steal a few checks from the bottom of the stack so I could cash them at local bars so I could drink. Beverly would only find out when the banks would call. Before long, I couldn't remember which bars I had written hot checks to, so I had to find new places to drink. We had gone bankrupt in an effort to start all over, but soon we were once again in debt up to our ears. Disaster loomed heavily.

In the course of the next year, I worked for seven different dealerships. Beverly was about to lose her mind, never knowing where I was working from one day to the next. Regardless of what dealership I was at, surprisingly enough, they all had the same problem—me.

I finally settled into a used car dealership called Auto World. It was owned by a guy with two first names, Charlie Frank. I thought that a little strange, but it was a job. The rumor was that Charlie had bought a bunch of "flood cars" from up in Pennsylvania and dried them out to sell to young sailors and people with bad credit. That was the word on the street. The sales staff of six was made up of a cast of characters who epitomized the vision of used car salesmen of the day.

Nicknames were supposed to be catchy and easy for customers to remember, so all six of us had our own, which were usually put on our business cards. Most of the names had been given to these guys over the years, based on some past behavior, habits, or previous career paths.

There was Docky-Wocky; he was my new hero. He had been a Navy hospital corpsman and was the image of a used car guy. He wore Polyester slacks, Ban-Lon shirts, white Cuban heeled shoes, and a big gold chain around his neck. He had a gruff voice from smoking big long cigars and drinking bourbon out of the bottle. He had a huge beer belly and because he was so overweight, he was always seemingly exhausted. Every few minutes he seemed to take a big breath and on his exhale, to no one in particular, he would exclaim, "Gawd damn!" He was the best deal closer I ever met.

"Fast Louie" had gotten his nickname because he talked so fast and never listened to a word anyone else said, including the customers. With machine-gun speed, he constantly walked around muttering," I'm talkin' 'bout talkin' 'bout, that's what I'm talkin' 'bout." He would even say this to the customers, who usually looked at him strangely, oblivious to what he was "talkin' 'bout." He didn't care. They seemed to follow him anywhere. It was really all about "come on inside and lets' see what we can do."

"Flaky Jake" was given his nickname because he was always stoned from taking some kind of drugs and was as nutty as fruitcake. He would often come out of the bathroom with a big "shit eating" grin on his face and white, flaky stuff coming out of his nose. When questioned about it, he would respond that he had just brushed his teeth. Docky would suggest, "Gawd damn, Jake. You might want to try and keep that toothbrush out of your nose."

The real name of "Ribbs No Fibbs" was Ribs Fibbs. He was an accountant-type guy who had been a big-time coin collector. He sold cars with gloves on because he had used so much acid in cleaning coins that his fingers were all eaten up and disfigured. It looked like he had leprosy. When he talked, people could actually understand him, and he made the deal seem like it was the most important thing that was ever going to occur in their lives.

"Stanley the Dropper," as the story goes, had gotten his nickname in the penitentiary. He had been arrested numerous times for dropping transmissions out of various muscle cars and selling them to junk dealers. When he finally got sent away, some of the other cons asked him what he was in for and when he told them, he was given his nickname.

And then there was me, "Clean Gene." I'm not sure why, but Fast Louie hung this nickname on me. It probably had to do with the fact that I was so naive about how they operated that they felt I was still "clean." This would change, and I would soon start fitting in.

I was always amazed at how these guys could live lives of reckless abandon and still seem to be successful. All of them were divorced and had left a trail of wrecked homes in their wakes, but strangely enough, I wanted what they had. The problem, of course, was that I was married and supposed to be a good husband and father. The two couldn't coexist. I was almost never going home. I loved Beverly and worshipped my little girl, but the need to drink without hindrance and the environment I was working in took precedence over everything else.

If there was ever an environment in which drinking was condoned, Auto World was the place. Work would end and we would head to the Lido Inn, where we would drink until 2:00 a.m. and then be off to an after-hours club until about four or five. I would then drive home, usually with one eye closed, often forgetting where I was or where I was going. The wrath of Beverly was the only thing I could be sure of. In fact, one night while I was passed out, Beverly was so angry that she stood over my drunken body and smashed the alarm clock radio on top of my head. I somewhat came to and saw this feisty five-foot-tall woman standing over me on the bed, staring at me with rage in her eyes. She then got dressed for work and took Amy to the baby-sitter's, and I was left with my standard sense of guilt and worthlessness.

This went on for a couple of more months, always with the most sincere new promises. I tried a couple of more psychologists and various doctors to see if there was a miracle cure for me out there. Without being totally drunk, the panic attacks came back. We had no insurance, so I was starting to visit the public health doctors. One psychologist, Dr. Fathy Abdou, was a dream interpreter. After sharing with him some of my behavior problems, he stated, "That's not a public health problem." I didn't know what he meant, but since I never dreamed because I was always passed out, I would try to make up what I thought I should be dreaming about. I managed to make up some really bizarre dreams, and I would be spurred on as I saw his eyes widen. He may have seen right through me. We never discussed drinking. As a last resort, I agreed to see Beverly's family doctor. After finding out where he was located, I found myself sitting in my car behind his office, fearful of dying.

chapter 20

No Victims Allowed

D r. Hubbard had been Beverly's family's doctor for many years, and after some time I finally went in to see if maybe he had the answer. Every time I went to see a shrink, I would always give him the *Reader's Digest* version of my problem, seeking a quick fix. It always went the same way, and even though Dr. Hubbard was only a family practice doctor, I thought it should be no different. After sitting down, he asked me, "What's going on?" I explained to him that I thought my panic may be caused by the marines, Vietnam, my alcoholic mother, the Catholic church, and so on.

He listened intently, and when I finished, I said, "So what do you think?" He said, "About what?" "About what I just told you," I quipped. His response was not what I was looking for. He looked me dead in the eye, smiled, and said, "I think you're spoiled." I thought, *Spoiled? You haven't been listening to a thing I've said.* Apparently he sensed my astonishment because his next comments helped change my life. He stated, "What you have just described to me is life; I listen to it all the time. Your problem is you don't think you're supposed to go through any of it, and that's a bigger problem." He then continued, "With all the stuff you are struggling with, I'm going to recommend you undergo domiciliary care at the state hospital in Williamsburg, Virginia." "Does that mean

I would have to live there?" I asked. "Yes, for a while," he stated. I thanked him and told him I would get back to him.

Little did I realize it at the time, but Dr. Hubbard had stolen my victimhood from me. I immediately left his office mumbling to myself, "That's what happens when you go to a family doctor for psychological problems," and I promptly went and got a beer. I really felt doomed. *State hospital. You got to be kidding.* It became apparent that I was going to have to treat this myself with cold beer until a miracle happened. I was smart enough to reason that I had to get away from mentally destroying my family and bringing continued chaos into my little girl's life. At least her relatives could offer her more stability than I could. Within a month, I just disappeared. It was the saddest day of my life.

Over the course of the next few months, I started hanging out with some old drunk and crazy high school buddies of mine. I knew I couldn't keep a job, and they would always let me crash at one of their houses. Most of their lives were in turmoil or they had already destroyed their own marriages with their sheer wild behavior. We went through a lot of drinking and fighting at various bars across town, and we often would appear as witnesses for one another to keep anyone from doing any long-term jail time. Many of them were doing drugs, but after a few pot-smoking attempts, I concluded it wasn't for me. It interfered with the type of booze-induced high I was accustomed to.

I knew Beverly was going to take action to get a divorce and have me pay child support if she could find me, so I tried to stay hidden as much as possible. I missed Amy terribly but since I couldn't keep a job, child support was going to be out of the question. Thank God for her relatives. Sometimes I would work under the table with one of the guys for a few bucks to drink on, and oftentimes they would just give me money to keep me hanging around. I took a job selling Kirby vacuum cleaners door to door for a few months, but because it was night work I couldn't keep it long. I started showing up at my appointments too drunk to make the presentation.

A few of us joined a rugby team and traveled with some of the former high school and college stars to play two-day tournaments across the South. Rugby is a sport that allows players to vent a little anger, and I used it for a catharsis. It was also good to see that I could play with these guys and even excel sometimes in spite of being hung-over from the previous night's drinking. It strangely verified what I had thought when I was in school—that I could play with these guys if I hadn't had to work.

Every now and then I would call Beverly just to see how Amy was doing. Once, I found out that she had taken a fall in the back seat of Bev's car and severely cut her leg on something. She required numerous stitches and a cast, and I felt horrible that I hadn't been there. I took a job at a gas station near the bar I hung out in and promised to start paying some support if I could spend some time with Amy. Bev agreed, and for a few months I was able to use my buddy's car and pick her up for a few hours and take her off with me. Of course, we went to Brad's Lounge, and she watched me drink while I showed her off. She was my brown-eyed angel even with a cast on. We really enjoyed those afternoons together, but time was running out for me at the gas station. It was interfering with my drinking.

It was early 1970, and after a couple of months I left the gas station and disappeared again, this time heading down to Virginia Beach. Even my buddies were starting to suggest that I drank too much. As I hitchhiked to the beach, I reasoned that I could probably get a job as a waiter during the summer. I thought I could make some good money each day and then be free to drink at night. I heard that waiters at fancy restaurants made really good money, so off I went on my job search. As long as I maintained a good bit of alcohol in my system, I could act somewhat stable. I had gotten a room in the remodeled garage of a home near the beach for twenty-five dollars a week.

chapter 21

1970: Gay Waiters
and the Marine

My first interview was at the fanciest restaurant at the beach. The Copper Kettle restaurant sat right on the boardwalk, and every table overlooked the Atlantic Ocean. They only served one meal—dinner—and each waiter had to wear an abbreviated tux. During the interview, I got the impression that the maître d', Ted, was a little gay, or as we used to joke, "light in his loafers," but that was okay. He seemed to like me and offered me the job right away. I had never heard that waiters at fancy restaurants were often gay, but it wouldn't have mattered to me; I was there for the drinking money. Besides, I enjoyed being around gay people.

They were a trip to be around and an even bigger trip to work with. I was told to be there the next day with black slacks and black shoes and socks; the restaurant would issue me the bow tie and tux jacket when I got to work.

The next day, another fellow, Mike, who had recently graduated from East Carolina University, and I were going to be the new servers. During the interview, I had told the maître d' about my experience as a marine and a salesman, so when it was time to introduce us to the other waiters, he daintily went through the restaurant clapping his hands and shouting, "Everyone! Everyone! Come up front to meet the new servers." It's not an exaggeration to say that within seconds; eight of the most "flaming homosexuals" in Virginia Beach came bounding out into the foyer to welcome us aboard. As Ted was introducing us, he said, "Now, Michael is a recent grad from East Carolina, and you know what they say about East Carolina boys. And Gene ... is a marine." Well, in a matter of seconds and after a few *ahh*s, this one waiter, Earl, came up beside me and said, "My God, girls. A marine." I had no idea what I was in for, but I had a feeling it was going to be a good ride.

It took about two days to figure out this waiter stuff, and I found out I was pretty good at it. Mike had asked me to be his roommate and he was a big beer drinker, so we were a natural fit. We were the only two straight waiters on staff. Roger, the chef, was a Philippine fellow who was glad to have us there. I quickly discovered that gay men are very picky about things being perfect, and the kitchen often took on the look of a madhouse with bickering and complaining all night long.

I soon found out that if I would bring Roger and the other kitchen staff, all Filipinos, cold soft drinks throughout the night, I would get treated great and my meals would get preferential treatment. As usual, everything seems to have an angle.

Before long, I started playing roles with the customers and would often talk with different accents at each table. The people loved it. Sometimes I would talk like a Brit when taking their orders and change to a Southern gentleman when I served them. I was having a ball. The place would close by about eleven, and with a couple hundred dollars in our pockets, Mike and I would go out drinking until the bars closed. We would then stagger to our apartment and keep the party going until we passed out or, if lucky, ended up in a hotel with some tourist girls, waking up by about eleven the next morning. I'd spend about three hours on the beach and then go home to shower and put on my tux. I had a great tan and looked the part of a real beach boy.

After getting a little more comfortable with my new surroundings, I even started doing a bit of drinking at work as the night wore on. I would often drink the rest of customers' drinks when they left after dinner. As time went on, this turned into a regular occurrence, and by about nine o'clock, when the last tables were seated, I was pretty much tanked. One evening I was so drunk that as I was serving a flaming beef kabob, I almost set the restaurant on fire. Not really, but Earl tells it that way.

The idea was to dab the beef kabob, which was on a long skewer with a highly flammable cotton ball full of flambé. By using two forks held together (it was called French service), we waiters would pick up the flaming cotton ball and dab the beef, temporarily setting it ablaze. The tables of the restaurant overlooked the ocean, and the scene was beautiful both inside and out. It was designed to be quite a spectacle, and it was on this night. As I was doing my drunken dabbing, with everyone looking on, and using my best French accent, some of the flaming flambé dripped onto the table and immediately set the paper napkins that the drinks were sitting on ablaze. A few of the other waiters started overreacting with screams of "Oh, my God!" as they scurried about and then tried to help by dousing the flames with water, which sent more flames shooting across the table. I finally smothered all of the flames with the linen napkins and all was well, sort of. I tried to discourage customers from ordering the beef kabobs from then on.

Mike and I were so well liked and open-minded about the gay community that we were even invited to the annual Drag Queen Ball in Norfolk one evening. We were given a front row table, and we had a blast. Looking at our gay friends all dressed up as women and performing songs and dances on stage was a sight to behold. To this day, I think I saw the best Liza Minnelli impersonation ever put on. Earl even introduced me from the stage as "Gene the Marine."

Things were going about as well as could be expected, and my drinking was somehow part of the beach scene we lived in. But I knew it wouldn't last forever.

✳

Beverly had no idea where I was, and I know she had once again gotten a divorce finalized. The summer was going to end, and eventually I would be faced with the reality that I couldn't hold a job where I couldn't drink all the time.

One afternoon as I was casually walking down the boardwalk on my way to work, I was suddenly startled by a car that drove up on the boardwalk and headed right toward me. It stopped just short of running me over; I didn't know what was going on. It was soon discovered that Beverly had spotted me and was attempting to get my attention. At least that was what she told the cop who was walking on the boardwalk at the time. After talking to her, he came over to me and mentioned that she may have been doing a little drinking herself and said that it might be best if I would take her home.

I'm not quite sure why it works this way, but as mentioned before, screwed-up men often seem to be very attractive to a certain type of woman and vice versa. When they get together, you can almost feel the suction as they are somehow magnetically drawn to each other. Whether it's love or not is a question for the shrinks, but it sure worked that way with Beverly and me.

As I was driving her home, to her parents' house, we started the same dialogue we had every time we were somehow reunited. I did my best to offer a feeble apology, followed by a futile attempt to make her understand my reasons for deserting her and my daughter.

*

The romance once again began to blossom with renewed intensity, and the promises of a different life "this time" were once again made. Hope was in the air once more, and even making love under these conditions was exhilarating. In spite of the fact that I could always talk a good game when I was drinking and flirting, most of the time my sexual prowess was questionable. My romantic qualities were usually minimal because of the drunken state I was always in prior to ending up in someone else's bed. But with Beverly, this set of circumstances always seemed to "fire me up."

There always had been a huge part of me that constantly missed Amy. This boardwalk incident, I reasoned, was perhaps part of Gods' plan. Beverly and I started talking about reuniting yet again. The problem, of course, was that we were now divorced, and Beverly said she was not going to "shack up," nor was she going to be married to a waiter.

chapter 22

December 1970: The Beer Man—I Was a Natural

With my work/drinking dilemma, I somehow managed to get a job driving a Schlitz Beer truck. To this day I don't know who steered me to this new career. But I knew they made good money, and I guess the easy availability of brew appealed to me. Anyway, I got the job.

As was usually the case, I excelled and my route became one of the best in the company. Each route salesman had the option of taking a helper with him when making the day's deliveries, and the helper would be paid by the salesman at the end of the day's work.

All of the helpers were black in those days, and each morning I could see and hear them talking out front in their "jive" language that no one but they seemed to understand. I thought it was so cool and often liked to hang with them when we came in after deliveries just to listen and make my futile attempt at talking like one of them. This was 1970, and even though socially-condoned racism was still somewhat prevalent, these guys seemed to be oblivious to it as they hung out in front of the warehouse. They even seemed to have a freedom and looseness that none of us had, and I admired that. They also took great pride in the fact that we had a couple of black salesmen and the first black supervisor in our market area. Robert Heinmann, the distributor and owner, was a good man and a pioneer in crossing color lines. If you were good at your job, that's all that mattered.

Most of the salesmen chose strong, young helpers. They would do most of the labor, and the driver could get his deliveries done quickly, return to the warehouse, check in, and be gone. I chose "My Man Jimmy." Jimmy was an illiterate, overweight fellow with jet black skin, a big afro, and only his two eye teeth. I don't know if he ever bathed, but he certainly didn't smell like it. He was impossible to understand when he talked and as slow as a snail, but what a character. No one ever chose Jimmy, but I guess my grandmother was calling out to me, so he became my guy. Sometimes Jimmy would ask me to pay him some of his money before we started the day's work so he could get a snack at the first stop. At first I refused, but then he would move so slowly and pout that I would finally give in.

Once we started deliveries, I would start drinking. I often had a sixteen-ounce beer in my lap as I was driving that huge beer truck. Jimmy never said a word, but he did give me a few strange looks with those big white eyes when we would have a close call on the road. One time I was so drunk by noon that we almost hit an airplane on the naval air station base. Jimmy would have gotten out of the truck if he could have found his way home. It normally would take six hours to make my deliveries, but with my drinking and Jimmy's slowness, it took about ten. I just don't know why I'm attracted to these "wounded ducks." Maybe he saw me as the one who was wounded, but I wouldn't have traded him for anybody else. He had a chance to make a few bucks and we had a good time together—until I got promoted.

Oftentimes the most productive route salesmen are chosen to be supervisors. Each supervisor is responsible for the production of eight to fifteen routes, and I had about twelve salesmen in my division. We were commonly referred to as the "beer man" when we went into a bar, and we would usually buy everyone in the place a round of Schlitz Beer. We wore suits and ties and were certainly well liked by all the customers. We also had a fat expense account to use as well as a company car.

I was doing so well by this time that Beverly and I decided to reunite and get remarried for the third time. I had joined the Jaycees, a young business and professional leaders association, and was starting to look like an honorable member of society. I was also committed to give this husband-and-father thing my best shot. I was still drinking but somehow managed to structure things so I could get through each day. I mean, after all, when I bought the bar a round, I certainly wasn't going to drink tea.

*

So, I usually had a steady buzz on. In fact, I had even convinced myself that it was my job to drink. Needless to say I excelled at this job. This too would soon change.

It was budget- and objective-making time for the company, and on one particular day, I had told all of my salesmen to meet me at the office at 4:00 to go over their objectives. When 4:00 came around, they were there to meet me, but I was not there. I was in one of my bars shooting pool in a tournament and was pretty much boozed up, so I was in no shape to go back to work. I called the office and told the secretary to cancel the meeting, to which she replied, "Mr. Heinmann wants to talk to you." He asked me what was going on, and I lied, saying the job was just too much pressure and if he wanted to come get the company car, he could. He did. Just like that, I quit this great job so that I could stay and drink. I had been there for three and a half years and our family life was starting to come together, and then …

As I staggered the one and a half miles home in the rain at two o'clock in the morning and fell in through the front door of the house, Beverly was there to greet me, but this time it was different. There wasn't any yelling, screaming, crying, or any of that—only resignation. When I told her I had quit my job, she sighed, looked at me with disgust, and said, "Whatever." Then she went to bed. I knew it was about over for us then. She was pregnant with our son, Jason, conceived after one of those "new resolve" lovemaking sessions, but it didn't matter. I was on a rapid descent downhill, and I knew it.

Within a few days, I somehow managed to get a Virginia State sales manager's job with the Mogen David wine company. In the interview, the guy asked me if I would meet him at the hotel bar.

He had flown in from Chicago. After we met, he asked if I wanted a beer or something, and I responded, "No, thanks. It's a little early for me, and I don't usually drink until the workday is over." I instantly got the job. He went back to Chicago, and I drank for the next two months day in and day out. He finally flew into Norfolk and asked me if I would pick him up at the airport. I immediately noticed that he had no luggage and, without leaving the airport, he said, "Have a seat." I sat down, and he said, "You're fired." He then stood up, turned his back to me, and walked away. It was the first job I had ever been fired from.

chapter 23

The Surrender Begins, Slowly

I drove around drunk for about three days, and finally in April of 1975, I checked myself in to the local psychiatric hospital. I was afraid to go home because I knew it was over. I didn't want to put Amy through any more confusion, and I knew I had failed at being the dad she deserved in her life.

It was about midnight, and I was standing out in front of the Tidewater Psychiatric Hospital (TPI) with a bottle of moonshine I had gotten from somewhere. After thirty uneventful days inside—save the times I would leave for a few hours after pottery, art therapy, or whatever and come back drunk—I finally was discharged.

✻

By then I had resigned myself to just being a drunk and waiting to see what happened to guys like me. Beverly had taken the car and moved herself and Amy out of the house we were renting and back in with her parents. The house was locked up tight because we hadn't paid the rent for a couple of months, and I headed back down to Virginia Beach to see if I could decide on my next move.

I called a buddy of mine from the beer business, and he agreed to let me stay at his place for a couple of weeks. We had been drinking buddies before, and after he got off of work, he would take me out drinking with him. I was out of money, but he was still working as a supervisor for Schlitz and was single, so he had plenty of money. He would go to work, and I would wander around the neighborhood stealing wine from the local stores to hold me over until he got home.

It wasn't long before he told me I couldn't stay there anymore because he had gotten a new girlfriend and she was moving in. He also was starting to notice my rather bizarre behavior, which was getting increasingly bizarre. Sometimes he would come home from a date and find me passed out in the bushes in front of his apartment. I was hiding from the world and didn't want the neighbors to see me, but I had nowhere else to go. And ... I had to drink.

Before long I started wandering down to "the Beach," and my heroes became the boys of the all-night Laundromat. These were guys with nicknames like Skilly Fry, High Test, Mumbles, and a guy I liked to call Dead Fred. This was a cast of real winos who had been on the street for years.

But there was a difference between them and me—they didn't seem to need to drink like I did. They would take it if it was available, but I had to have it. The all-night Laundromat afforded the drunks a place to stay without bothering the tourists during the summer and a warm place late at night during the cold months. I was only on the street with these guys for a short time, and Dr. Hubbard's recommendation of the state hospital started bouncing around in my mind. Maybe I did need to be put away.

When I would go too long without a drink, I would start getting terrible delirium tremens, or DTs, so I was always looking for somewhere to steal alcohol. I would walk along the outside balconies of hotels and sift through the maids' carts as they were inside the rooms, looking for remnants of bottles that were left after the previous night's partying. Convenience stores and grocery stores would provide the best opportunities. Drunks are pretty creative when it comes to drinking. It was the days before cameras were everywhere. In the grocery stores, I could go in, get a cart, and act like I was shopping. I would pick up a bottle of wine, go around to a vacant aisle, and lean into a shelf, where I would down the bottle quickly and then nonchalantly leave the cart as if I realized I had left my money at home. Of course, I was watched closely in some stores because I hadn't bathed and it was obvious that I wasn't there to buy shampoo and toothpaste. So I had to be a little picky. I never got caught. It seems I was somehow being allowed by God or the "law of the universe" to slowly kill myself. It was working too.

While I had been in TPI, another patient in my group named Bob watched me going in and out and coming back drunk. One morning during group therapy, as I was taking the heat from the group for my behavior, he asked, "How much do you drink?" I became very defensive and said, "What's that got to do with anything?" His response rang in my ear: "Well, I'm an alcoholic, and now I'm in here for depression because I stopped going to my twelve-step meetings, but we got a lot of flaky cats like you in my recovery group." I followed with, "I might be a lot of things, but I ain't no alcoholic." But a seed had been planted. Every time I took a drink after that, I saw that guy's face.

When I got out of that hospital, I kept hearing those words, and it was becoming apparent that there was an outside chance—perhaps, in spite of how cool I really was, that perhaps, just perhaps—maybe he was right. Maybe alcohol was a problem.

On Christmas morning of 1975, I experienced my greatest fear. I was doing my standard walk around the outskirts of Virginia Beach, trying to figure out what was going to be my first target to steal my wine from. The nearest 7/11 store seemed like a safe bet. I walked around the side of the building with a bottle of Mad Dog wine tucked safely in my trousers. I preferred Mad Dog or Wild Irish Rose wine; however, when you're on the street, you don't really care. I used to joke that when you drink mad-dog you never have to go to the bathroom, you just walk around leaking all the time. As I tried to unscrew the top, my hands started trembling, and it was obvious that I had better get some of this down before I went into a full-blown convulsion. I was hurting real bad, and the alcoholic "madness" was upon me.

Lifting the bottle up to my lips, I gulped and gulped until the entire pint was gone and then waited for the few moments of relief that usually followed. Nothing happened—no relief, no buzz, nothing. I knew I was screwed. I had heard that there would come a time when even the booze stopped working. That time had come, and I knew I needed help.

I called my old Schlitz friend Bill and asked him if I could use his house to call the local recovery group and get myself some help. He was more than happy to help me, if I was serious, but asked that I not mess up his house. I hadn't bathed in quite some time so he had some concerns. He wasn't going to be home but said he would leave the door unlocked.

When I made the call, the guy who answered opened with, "Merry Christmas, how can I help you?" I responded by saying, "My name is Gene, and I think I have a problem with drinking a little too much wine." His words took me by surprise when he said, "Well, that's great. You're my Christmas present. In fact, I got a couple of guys sitting around here waiting for a live one. How about I send one of them out to see you?" I thought to myself, *What a bunch of losers, if I'm their Christmas present.* Hesitantly, I agreed and gave him directions.

Within a half hour, I was in full DTs and sweating profusely. I'm not sure why, but whenever I was in DTs, I would hear babies crying and train whistles blowing. By the time "Big Tom" got there, I was about to lose my mind.

*

There was a thundering knock on this big aluminum door that I had propped open before I went and sat on the floor in the corner of the apartment, not knowing what to expect. I pitifully uttered, "Come in."

Big Tom was a giant of a man. He stood about six feet, eight inches; weighed about three hundred pounds; was wearing bib overalls; and was carrying a banjo. I thought I was hallucinating. As he looked around the room, he finally spotted me and smiled before saying, "Well, damn, Bubba. I'll bet nobody's told you that they love you lately, have they?" I thought, *Jesus, this is the story of my life. Here I am—a divorced, cowardly, Catholic drunk—and I finally call the alcoholic hotline and they send me out this six-foot-eight, three hundred pound homosexual who tells me he loves me.* Tom must have known what I was thinking because he followed up with, "No, Bubba, I love ya just like you are right now. You'll be a lot tougher to love once you get all cleaned up."

I was soon to discover that recovering alcoholics stay sober by helping other alcoholics get sober. That impressed me, and it was believable. I knew that at this stage of my life, I wasn't going to do anything for someone else unless there was something in it for me.

Tom led me downstairs and told me to get in the back of the pickup. He had another fellow named Phil sitting in the front, and he was drunker than me. I thought, *Maybe this guy is the official guy on Christmas who just goes out rounding up drunks and taking them to their doom, sort of like the town crier during the Plague who yelled, "Bring out your dead!"*

*

Tom explained it was still a little early for the meeting so we were going to go over to Melba's house and wait for the meeting to start.

Melba was an old lady who didn't have a drinking problem but just seemed to like having crazy people around her. As we walked up the stairs to her townhouse, it wasn't long before I was sitting at the dining room table sweating like a pig while Big Tom and Phil started picking and plucking their musical instruments. I had no idea how, but Phil had produced a guitar from somewhere. He couldn't play a lick, but he was shaking so bad that he was making some sort of noise and Tom was trying to chime right in with him. It was the loudest racket I ever heard. My ears were ringing so loudly that I thought my head was going to explode. *So this is what hell is really like.*

Melba seemed to be relishing the concert as she sat smiling and rocking in her rocking chair. She looked over at me and said, "See, if you quit drinking you can have fun like this too." I feared I was losing my mind.

Tom then took me to my first recovery group meeting. When I walked in, I spotted a beautiful redhead, and immediately my whole routine changed. She looked sane and was gorgeous, so without any hesitation I headed over to her with my usual "cool " swagger, scraped the food debris off of my shirt, and said, "Hey, baby. What's happening?" Pretty Mary looked at me, took a whiff, smiled, and said, "Keep coming back" before she swiftly walked away. I thought, *She'll be back, once she finds out I'm a marine.*

I found out later that she was the head of the math department for one of the state's largest school districts. I never did see Phil again, but after the meeting Tom and another fellow tried their best to help me get my life back on track.

Big Tom was right. After getting my mom and dad to agree to let me stay at their house for a couple of weeks, I started feeling pretty good. My health came back quickly, and I got a job washing dishes. Tom said it was important to stay busy. After a couple of weeks, I got a room with the son of a friend of my dad's. Things were looking up.

Before long I started thinking, *Maybe it wasn't that bad.* Then I went to a party I shouldn't have gone to and was off to the races again. But then I knew what was wrong with me. For the next ten months I went in and out of a couple of detoxes. Ironically, they were part of the state hospital. I often thought about Dr. Hubbard and what he had said years before. One of the detoxes even provided mouthwash in the little bag of plastic toiletries, and believe it or not, the Cepacol mouthwash had alcohol in it. After getting caught with empty bottles of the other patients' Cepacol, I was patiently informed that if it happened again, I would be kicked out. After about five days, most of the alcohol was out of my system, and a few days later I was directed to another recovery group.

I went to the groups religiously for about—you got it—ninety days. I even got a job with the local Ford dealer. Pretty soon, I was feeling so good that I once again started questioning how bad it had been.

Maybe I'm not an alcoholic, I told myself. *I mean, check it out—I got a good job selling cars again, and I look good, and I'm playing racquetball to keep in shape. My ears are still ringing but, what the hell, and the panic attacks have subsided. I probably could get away with having a few beers with some of the guys. I mean, after all, I'm only twenty-nine years old, way too young to be an alcoholic.* I finally convinced myself that it had all been a terrible misunderstanding.

It was a Saturday afternoon when I slipped away a little early from Kimnach Ford. The company had given me a nice 1976 Ford Mustang for a demo car, and I must admit I was looking pretty cool. My first stop was the liquor store, where my cool look would be matched shortly by my cool feeling. Walking in the front door of the store, I couldn't help but look around to see if any of my new recovery friends spotted me. Naturally, I hadn't had time to tell everyone about the misunderstanding.

Without going into too much detail, suffice it to say that within a couple of hours, I had gotten completely drunk, gotten into a fight, and was back on the street. But this time, I believe I was convinced. The terrible misunderstanding was in my own head and only there. Alcoholics are like that. They see and hear what they want to see and hear, whether it's real or not.

chapter 24

Reborn: October 29, 1976

A friend of mine named Wiley saw me on the street and asked me if I wanted to stay at his and his girlfriend's place for a few days to "dry out" again. Grateful, I said yes. After sitting up all night shaking uncontrollably, I realized I couldn't do it. At about six o'clock in the morning, while everyone was asleep, I sneaked up to his bedroom, took his girlfriend's keys, and headed to the nearest 7/11 store. I didn't have any money, but that didn't concern me; I was there to steal a bottle of wine. I walked into the store and grabbed a couple of bottles of Mad Dog 20/20 wine out of the cooler. As I turned around, the clerk was staring right at me with alarm. After all, I was the only one in the store.

I was suddenly faced with the terrible dilemma of perhaps having to club this poor guy with one of the bottles so I could run outside and drink the other one. It was at that moment that I realized, *It has come to this.* To get a drink I might actually kill somebody. The conflict was huge because I needed a drink, but for some unknown reason I turned, put the bottles back, and walked outside.

The next thing I remember was a young Navy guy, who was also at Wiley's house that night, propping my head up and telling the rescue squad guys that he was going to take care of me. I had gone into convulsions from alcohol withdrawal, and the ambulance had been called; the paramedics thought I should go to the hospital. The Navy kid, who was in recovery himself, assured them that I had been in enough hospitals and that he would see that I got help. That morning, he and Wiley took me to a local recovery center called the Easy Does It Club and dropped me off, wishing me well. I oftentimes joke that up to that point in my life, I had been in about five different mental hospitals, and they had all diagnosed me differently. However, they were all probably accurate.

A wise old man named Elmo took me under his wing for a few days, and rather than sending me to another detox, he suggested that I sober up the old-fashioned way. A bottle of Karo syrup and a Nehi orange soda became my new drink of choice—his choice. I was told to sip it slowly, and supposedly the sugar content would help get my pancreas back in shape and help minimize the shakes. *Yuck*, I thought, but I had suddenly become teachable and started following everyone else's directions. "My way" was obviously not working.

chapter 25

Twelve Steps to Somewhere

P art of rebuilding your life according to Elmo and other wise old sages at the Easy Does It Club was to work through twelve steps, which are part of expelling the obsession to drink and at the same time cleaning up your past. This means going back to those you have harmed and making restitution wherever possible. I had a lot of restitution to make, financial and otherwise. The list was long. They talked about promises that would always materialize if we worked the steps properly. Being a car guy, it sounded like a guarantee. That's what I needed, a guarantee.

It was suggested that I take a simple job for the first few months, so I got another job washing dishes at a local steakhouse. I had no car, so I rode the bus or hitchhiked wherever I needed to go. My mom and dad graciously allowed me to stay at their house once again until I got on my feet, but they had some strict conditions. There would be no drinking, no asking them for a ride anywhere, and an 11:00 pm curfew. My dad assured me that if I broke any of these terms, I would be back on the street.

My mother had undergone a mastectomy for breast cancer back in 1971, and after a year of remission, the cancer had spread and she had been given six to nine months to live, so the family was a little on edge and didn't need any more excitement in their world. It was already 1976, and she seemed to be defying the odds. On my second night home, Mom was her usual dramatic, boozed-up self, and she informed me that she needed help to stop drinking too. I called one of my recovery friends, Johnnie J., and he suggested that she call Alcoholics Anonymous (AA) to ask for help. She did, and she never took another drink. She miraculously lived until 1984 when she died at the age of sixty. In fact, she outlived the oncologist who had given her six months to live back in 1972.

First on my list of amends and restitution were Beverly and her family. They had to rescue her so many times when I abandoned them. Then there was my brown-eyed angel, Amy. That was the most important one for me. She was only eight years old, and although I wasn't real confident in my ability to stay sober, I did the best I could to try to explain my past without promising anything to her except that I was going to try to be a good dad from then on.

In fact, now that I saw a glimmer of hope, I even tried to convince Beverly to give it one more chance. Understandably, she said no. She had heard it all before. We were divorced once again, and court-ordered child support was in effect.

Bob Heinmann, the beer distributor, was also on the list, as well as a few friends I had taken advantage of, and my parents, who stayed in a constant state of concern. I also had to go around to the various stores I had stolen from and watch the clerks' eyes widen as I tried to explain what I was doing and gave them money for stolen wine. I would always explain I had walked out without paying for something and needed to make things right. There was a comical side to it because they usually didn't know exactly what to do with the money. I sometimes walked out the door chuckling at *their* dilemma.

There were also a few car dealers and managers I was going to have to come clean with about why, at various times, I had taken their company cars and just disappeared. Little did I know this would prove to be a frightening and yet positive life-changing experience.

The dishwashing job didn't pay too well, and I knew I would have to get a better job if I was going to stay out of jail for non-support. Beverly had met a stable guy named Chip who was well educated and successful, had never been married, and welcomed the chance to have a family. In fact, Beverly was expecting my son, Jason, when they started dating, and she informed me that Chip was eager to adopt both Amy and Jason, eliminating the need for child support, if I would be willing to let that happen.

That idea may have seemed logical to anyone who had followed my usual pattern, but I never entertained the thought. I rejected the offer immediately. I was hopeful that someday we could have a good relationship. All I needed was to start making some money.

I was a little gun-shy about getting back into the car business. *Too much action and temptation*, I thought, so I steered away and tried all kinds of different things for those first few months. I tried everything from cleaning carpets to selling birdseed. I didn't make much money but managed to make enough to get an apartment with another guy in alcoholism recovery. I even bought me a little junk car to get to work. It was an old Nash Rambler with one headlight and no reverse but it was a car.

My first recovery mentor was a tough old bird named Ernie. He held me accountable to just keep showing up and quit questioning everything that didn't go the way I thought it should be going. He constantly reminded me that *my* best efforts at life had landed me on the street. With Ernie's prodding, I slowly developed the habit of just showing up. Of course, he had a little more direct way of suggesting it. His strategy to teach me humility was direct and to the point. He would say things like, "For a guy that doesn't know anything, you sure talk a lot." He would often look at me with an exasperated expression and exclaim, "Just show up and shut up." He told me to be where I'm supposed to be, when

I'm supposed to be there, and do the best I can at whatever it is I'm doing and quit worrying about results. *Okay, I can do that.*

Armed with this new philosophy, I was convinced that if my head was on right, I could work anywhere.

I decided that maybe I should give the car business another shot. After all, I had never tried it sober before, and who knows, maybe I'd be good at it for more than ninety days if I could keep from self-destructing. In addition my Rambler had finally died.

I got a sales job at that same local Ford dealership where I hadn't burned too many bridges and amazingly, by practicing the art of showing up each day, an interesting thing started happening. Not only was I being successful, but I started meeting some very interesting people and even started paying my child support on time. I took up racquetball once again, joined the company softball team, and with my usual vengeance, started getting in good physical shape.

Dad and Mom when they met around 1943

Grandpa…the Alderman, or whatever he was, holding me

Nana and Grandpa Turner and home during depression

Mom and Dad…always in love and at one of those officer parties

Me, four-years-old and lovin' life

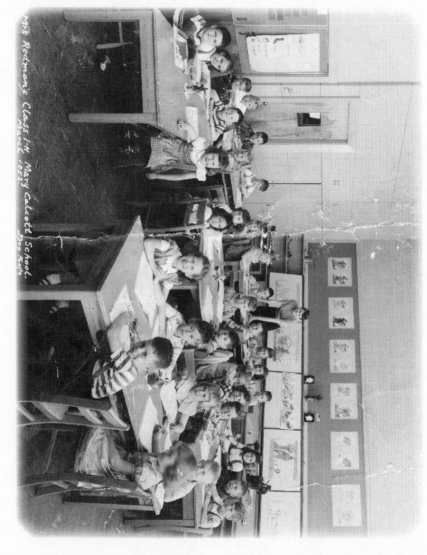

Mrs Redman and class—me in front and Dorothy Bradshaw at my side

Me, front middle, behind the catchers mitt. First Little league team.

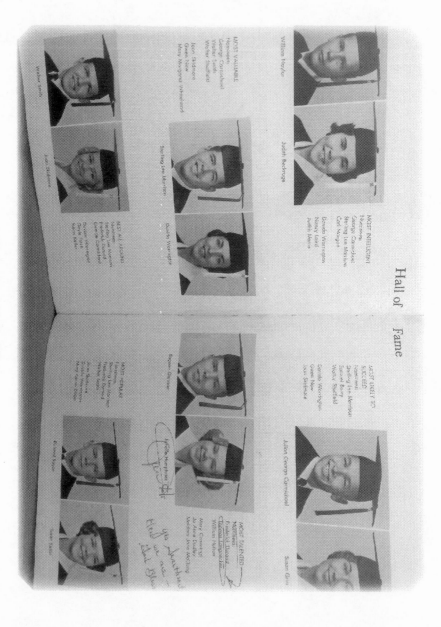

High school Hall of Fame

"The Best Dressed Seniors of '47"

Guess who the scarecrow is?

Kitty and Clarence in the early days

My boot camp photo

Kitty and Beverly before our first wedding

Beverly and I toasting

R.D. Williams…the greatest Marine I knew to my back right

Amy…my brown eyed angel

Jackie and I in the mountains on our last date

Dianne and I right after the wedding...notice her smile and 5 yrs later. Still smiling, a miracle.

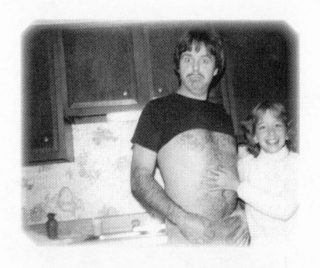

*Amy Marie…telling me to trim down Dad. My favorite
dance recital picture…both Amy's loved to dance.*

One of the Top Sales award before I had them taken down.

Kelly and Jason in their teen years

Amy Gee (for Gorman) as she looks today…lovely as ever.

Amy and Jason at the beach with the ol' man.

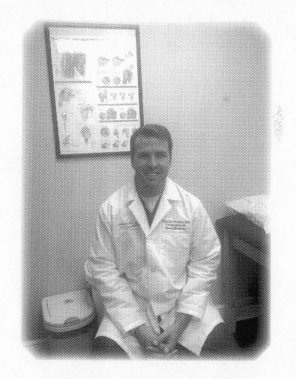

Dr Chad…proud papa, I am.

Chad's wife Amanda...the lawyer, with Dianne, the Big Boss.

Owen and his wife Aimee...who is also our Internet manager

Grandson Hunter and the grip of Kong

I'd give em away…but my wife won't let me…
Our successful slogan for our businesses.

All American Gabe celebrating his 100th wrestling victory

Gene and Dianne Gasman and their son Owen

Gene, Dianne, and Owen Gasman at the Dirt Cheap Auto location

Day of Golf with Dianne, and the three of us at Dirt cheap cars

Amy Marie Howe, Owen and Aimee Gorman and Pat Howe

Katie with the Katie's Kup Princess 2013

Tom Wright…business manager and friend

Shana and Jason, Chase's Mom and Dad.

Grandson Chase…let's sell some cars!

*My Green-eyed Angel Dianne and I taking
a break for an up-to-date photo*

Gene and Dianne, with Beverly and husband, Curtis

Grizzled old Author enjoying a good cigar

Reflecting on the Miracle.

chapter 26

1977: So Many Women, So Little Time

My good friend Eddie Williams took me aside one day and asked if I would do him a favor. He said he had been dating a girl named Dianne. He said he had sold her a car and taken her out a few times, but now he was going to get back with his wife and wanted this girl to meet someone nice. He also said she was drop-dead gorgeous, was very shy, had strict morals, and wasn't into the bar scene. Her ex-husband had been a drinker and womanizer, and that was what had broken up her previous marriage. He assured her that I was a good guy and, more important, that I didn't drink but was still a little crazy. Would I like to meet her?

Hmm, let me think about this. I was dating a beautiful blonde named Jackie, who was a big shot with the Navy Alcohol Treatment Program. She was also drop-dead gorgeous and had a master's degree. In my new circle of friends, my first "ego-feeding" thought was that I was the envy of many of my peers, and she certainly made me look good. But, what the hell—it was only a date, and I'd be glad to do my friend a favor and perhaps bring a little joy into this poor, damaged woman's life. "Okay, where do you want me to meet her?" I asked.

Eddie had the three of us meet at a local restaurant. The plan would be, after introducing us, he would excuse himself and let my effervescent charm and gift of gab take over. Being my usual cautious (perhaps *self-centered* is a better word) self under these type of conditions, I weaseled my way in the side door so I could take a look at her from afar and start making up my excuse, in case I needed to make a hasty retreat. Eddie was a good friend, but there was always the chance she wasn't quite as gorgeous as he had led me to believe. My suspicions soon vanished. Sitting across from Eddie was perhaps the most beautiful brunette I had ever seen—shoulder-length brown hair, beautiful green eyes, and a slender body with seemingly just the right proportions. She even had a little mole on the side of her cheek, which according to my mother was really a beauty mark that many women painted on their faces in the old days to make everything perfect. *Wow*, I thought. *I wonder what she saw in Eddie?*

After a quick introduction and some small talk about nothing in particular, Eddie excused himself and was out the door. It soon became apparent that this beautiful woman was not easily impressed with my personality and really didn't have much to say about anything that could keep a dialogue going. All I seemed to do was stare at her beauty and—being rigorously honest, I must admit—I was thinking about how good she would make me look when out in public. After all, it was still all about me. I even found myself attracted to the fact that she didn't talk much. I mean, how good can it get? A beautiful woman who doesn't talk much? I don't see a problem with that.

After about an hour of one-sided conversation, I realized I was quickly running out of things to say. I found out all I needed to know and half-heartedly made a date with her for later in the week. It was obvious that this pretty little Catholic girl had a lot of trust issues and was not going to be an easy conquest for my love/lust interests. This somehow intrigued me even more, and I knew

I would have to plan my strategy carefully if I was to score on our first date. But, there was a problem. My extreme self-centeredness was still in command of my life. With the feeling that I hadn't impressed her very much, I decided I needed to focus my attentions on Jackie. I guess I was trying to hedge my bet and didn't want to lose my beautiful counselor girlfriend in case Dianne was too uninterested to make something happen with us. I would soon find out that she wasn't as damaged as I thought.

✳

When I didn't show up or call the night of our date, this shy young girl showed her mettle. At this point, she didn't know just how self-centered and unreliable I was and had no idea how chaotic my past had been. Consequently, with her being extremely reliable, stable, and honest to the core, she was concerned about what had happened to me. That concern was soon replaced by anger. The following day, she figured she would look up my phone number and give me a piece of her mind. Unfortunately, she found Gene Gorman in the phone book, and when she called and blurted out, "Where were you last night?" my father responded, "I think you want my son." I had been sober only six months, was officially Gene Gorman *Jr.*, and certainly was not in any phone book.

After my dad gave her my phone number, she called and let me know how she felt about being stood up. She also made it a point to tell me that she had called my dad looking for me and embarrassed herself with the call. Now, I too suddenly felt embarrassed. I made some feeble excuse about being sick. The reality was that I *was* sick—with the disease of self-centeredness..

I was suddenly faced with another dilemma. Dianne's show of assertiveness was strangely attractive to me. Her display of self-respect pulled me in a direction that I had never envisioned. I was so attracted to this that I groveled to make another date, and she was just kind (or sick) enough to give me a second chance.

*

On our first real date, we went to a movie titled *Carrie*. It was one of those scary ones, and I'm not sure why we chose it. All I know is that at each sudden, scary moment, she would let out a little scream and grab my arm. It seemed like each time she touched my arm, it would set my internal chemistry off; I knew there was something going on. She still didn't talk too much, but progress was being made.

On the first date, I got not even a kiss, but the chemistry was there. That was enough for now. After all, she had been on a couple of dates with another guy from work, and I was still dating Jackie. Neither of us wanted to commit to each other quite yet, but we knew a strong attraction was there. For the time being, we decided to date on Saturdays and see where it went. There was a beautiful little six-year-old girl in the picture from her first marriage who garnered most of Dianne's attention when Dianne wasn't working. Her name was, as chance would have it, Amy, just like my own little girl.

chapter 27

Wearing My Oxygen Mask

Our next few dates involved a pizza or a movie but no kissing and certainly no lovemaking. *What's wrong with this girl?* My next strategy was to take her to watch me play softball for the City League Championship Team, which was sponsored by Kimnach Ford, where I was working at the time. Surely once Dianne saw what a "super jock" I was, she would fall head over heels and we would promptly find ourselves in the bedroom making mad, passionate love for the rest of our lives.

I played shortstop, and every time I made a play, I would look to the stands anticipating her cheering for my brilliant performance. Unfortunately, she was usually preoccupied with something else and not even watching me in action.

This was somewhat of a letdown, and I started feeling like there was nothing I could do to impress this woman. It never dawned on me that my job wasn't to impress her. She just wasn't interested in paying homage to this man who felt he deserved to be paid homage to. *Self-centeredness is a terrible thing*, I thought. What's a guy to do?

For some reason, she agreed to keep going to my softball games on our date night. I guess she felt safe. One particular game would change the whole picture before it even got started. As we were pulling into the parking lot, she noticed a plastic cup insert lying on the console of this little Ford Mustang. It's designed to fit in a jock strap and cover the genitals. It's hard plastic with about five or six holes in it for ventilation. I had left it there and only put it on when the game started because it's too uncomfortable to just wear around town. She had three brothers, so I assumed she knew what it was. When we stopped, she asked me, "What's this thing?" Not wanting to miss the chance, I said, "It's an oxygen mask." She replied, "An oxygen mask? How does it work?" This was too good to pass up. "Well, you just hold it up over your nose and mouth and breathe deeply. It's designed to keep you from hyperventilating. That's what the holes are for. Try it. You'll see what I mean." Of course, she tried it, and I told her she had to breathe five or six times to feel the effect. As fate would have it, three or four of my buddies were walking by and saw this beautiful new girlfriend of mine sniffing my "oxygen mask." They were quick to give me a raised-eyebrow smile and thumbs up. "That's what I'm talking about!" they shouted in unison. Right before I hit the field, I told her what it really was as I tucked it down my pants. I don't think she took her eyes off of me the whole game.

Falling in Love

Dianne and I had started the daily phone calls to each other just to check in, and one weekend I just sort of disappeared. I had the weekend off and, not feeling that I was being properly "worshipped," I took Jackie on a prearranged trip to the Great Smoky Mountains. I figured the chances for Dianne and me were slim, what with my being so self-absorbed, and I didn't want to lose Jackie. After all, she was also gorgeous and still thought I was cool and seemed to appreciate my personality and craziness. Unfortunately, I was not a good companion for that weekend.

I had fallen in love with Dianne and didn't realize it until I was away from her. When Dianne called my office, they informed her that I had gone to the mountains for three days. I think it was at this time that she found she had fallen in love with me. This turned the heat up on our relationship, and upon my return, we decided we would have to make a decision to be in a relationship together or stop seeing each other. Telling Jackie was tough, but she knew something was wrong after that weekend in the mountains. Dianne's job was a little easier, I assumed. All she had to do was convince the guy at the office that she appreciated the watch he had given her but that she was now going to be with me. I mean, who gives his date a watch anyway? It never dawned on me that some guys are just nice guys.

After making the commitment, I felt it was necessary to tell Dianne all about my past. I was a bit concerned that she would suddenly just get up and walk out, thinking, *This guy is not such a good catch after all.* I mean, I wouldn't have stuck around with me, so I assumed she wouldn't either.

We had talked a little about my alcohol problems, but now it was time to get it all out in the open. I covered it all—the mental hospitals, arrests for fighting, detoxes, divorces, and bankruptcies, and I even went back through my childhood days.

chapter 28

Harold Pennington

Harold Pennington was a serene and gentle man who had founded Serenity Circle, one of the recovery groups whose meetings that I attended. He was one of those people who seem to have that chemistry that just makes you feel better by being in their presence.

As I was working through the twelve steps, I asked him if he would be my sponsor. A sponsor, I was told, is someone who is willing to be there for you as you learn to deal with life on life's terms and guide you as you take each step. Harold had convinced me that to have an honest relationship, I couldn't hold anything back with someone I wanted to spend the rest of my life with.

He then went further and suggested that I start depending on a power greater than myself and start praying to that power on a regular basis. He didn't care what the power was but suggested that God would be a good name for it.

In order to move on in life in a healthy fashion, I was going to have to enlarge my spiritual life. If I didn't work on my humility, the chances were good that I would drink again. He reminded me that God will do for me what I can't do for myself, which means I have to do what I can. I started hitting my knees to pray each morning and each evening. In the mornings, I would read at least two pages of something spiritual before starting my day. The book *Sermon on the Mount* by Emmet Fox became my spiritual life manual; I have read it at least once every year for thirty-seven years as of this writing.

That night, I hit my knees and prayed sincerely for the first time in many years. I asked God to help me gain a stronger faith. Harold also harped on the fact that "when you do good things, good things happen in your life, and when you do bad things, bad things happen and that's just the way it is, whether you believe in God or not." I soon followed with, "What about when you're doing good and bad things happen anyway?" His answer was gentle but direct. "When you're doing good and bad things happen, there is some eventual good that will come out of it." Harold called it the "law of the universe."

✳

No matter what I told Dianne, she never judged me. In fact, as I opened up, she suddenly felt free to share her past. As mentioned earlier she had been in a relationship with a guy who was her high school sweetheart, but once he started doing drugs, he turned into a womanizer and became abusive, first mentally and, finally, physically. Once it became physical, she was out of there. She took Amy and moved in with her brother. Her husband did the usual begging for her to return and even lashed out at her as she was packing up her belongings, but she was not going to be intimidated into staying. I instantly knew I was with a very special and strong woman. In fact, *I* was intimidated. I wasn't sure I was worthy to have her as my soul mate. Actually, I *knew* I wasn't worthy. Strangely, I felt I would have to become worthy. This would be a never-ending task—I did know that.

Dianne had one of those stable jobs at the phone company, and as we dated I was still struggling with my self-centeredness. I kept changing jobs, thinking the grass was greener somewhere else. The truth was I kept taking the problem with me wherever I went because the problem was me!

I finally left the car business, and with this newfound sobriety, I became what my friends would call delusional. Since I was on a faith-based track, I thought I needed to try and find out what "spiritual mission" I was supposed to be on. I soon took a job at the Easy Does It Club, where I had met my mentors. The fact that I wouldn't be able to pay my child support on time never even came into the equation. It soon would.

After about three months, Beverly and my other creditors found out where I was, and soon the wage garnishes started coming into the office. I would tell Dianne about it, and she would often look at me with raised eyebrows but never said a word about all of these changes. We had made a commitment, and she took those kinds of things seriously. Although I never asked, it was also obvious she wasn't going to be paying off my garnishees or late child support.

It soon became apparent that I was going to have to get back into sales in order to stay out of jail, and I reluctantly contemplated going back in the car business. Then I got a phone call from my old friend Eddie Williams. After asking how Dianne was doing, he told me about this new company he was working for called Cox Broadcasting. It was 1978, and they had just acquired the local cable TV franchise and were selling cable TV subscriptions door to door. He wanted to know if I would like to interview for a job. He said they were making good money and thought I would be good at it. *Hmm, door-to-door sales, eh? Sounds like something I might be qualified to do.* The next day, I was interviewing with the sales manager, a typical, upbeat, positive type, and after telling him about my previous sales experience, I got the job.

Selling cable TV was like shooting fish in a barrel. Each sales rep was given a stack of fifty to one hundred three-by-five index cards with street names and addresses on them. The idea was to follow the same streets where the cable television lines were going to be hung on the utility poles and sign people up for the basic cable service. The cost to sign up was $10 and then $7.50 per month for as long as the subscriber kept the service or, as we used to joke, the rest of their lives.

The cable would make TV pictures excellent, making old TVs seem brand new. In addition, the subscriber would get approximately twenty channels instead of the three available without cable. It was just too easy. We went to work at 2:00 in the afternoon and turned in the previous day's paperwork. Then, after a brief sales meeting, we hit the street and waited for people to come home from work so we could sign them up. We were usually finished by 8:00 pm. The best part was, we got to keep all of the money we collected at sign up as our commission. So if I signed up ten people, I made a hundred dollars. I seemed to be good at this, so I was signing up fifteen to thirty a day, sort of like selling Christmas cards. *Wow, maybe Harold was right.*

I was making good money, and my confidence was at an all-time high. All I was doing was showing up, just like I had been told. It was a little surprising to me that I seemed to do so much better than most of my coworkers. The fact was that I was showing up every day with a good attitude, and most of them couldn't even show up every day. Staying active in regular recovery meetings and working with others seemed to be an antidote for negative thinking. I guess my work ethic had been established early on in my life, and being sober was allowing it to flourish. Hell, I was grateful to be alive and not locked up in a mental hospital. Life was starting to make sense to me.

One of the many habits I had acquired from Harold to get my head right before starting me daily sales routine was reading two pages a day of something spiritual before I went to work. I would usually stop in a church somewhere near the neighborhood where I was going to be selling . On this particular day the nearest church was a synagogue. I had never been in one of them so I felt it might be a unique experience. I tried the doors and the only one open was on the side of this large temple.

After going inside it was obvious it was a small chapel type room with pews and an altar type table where the rabbi usually stands. I was alone and sat right up front and started reading my book. It was around three in the afternoon and before long a few older men shuffled in and sat in the back pews. Soon there was a "psssst..pssst." I turned and one of the men patted his head and loudly whispered "Yamaka." I whispered back "I don't have one." He then pointed to the door and said there were some in the bag outside. I then got a yamaka, placed it on my head and returned to my seat, proudly relishing the non-denominational moment I was displaying.

A minute later a Rabbi came in carrying the Torah. I started getting a little nervous. He looked at this new member of his congregation sitting up front and smiled as he asked "Do you want to help me with the afternoon prayers?" I told him I would but I was Catholic and don't know what to do. The back row started mumbling loudly and the poor Rabbi didn't know what to say. He finally said "maybe you better not stay." I agreed and returned my yamaka to the bag, smiled and walked out. I told my Jewish friend Sybil the story and unknown to me she promptly called the Rabbi. He assured her I caught everyone by surprise and he would be happy to have me visit the synagogue anytime.

Harold kept telling me that the law of the universe was at work and that as long as I kept sowing, I would keep reaping. He had encouraged me to keep reading and studying *The Sermon on the Mount* by Emmet Fox. It is a realistic look at what Jesus and other religious leaders taught and how it can be applied to everyday life. Best of all, it suggests that each reader decide what he or she wants to believe instead of what he or she *ought* to believe. Although I had been raised Catholic, I never felt like I had any kind of relationship with a god. All of my religious upbringing as a child had been done under duress, and my god for the past twelve years had really been King Alcohol. As previously mentioned, I devoured the book, and it was another turning point in my life.

With this newfound freedom and stability, Dianne and I started talking about marriage. We both believed we should get married if we were in this for the long haul, especially since we wanted to have children together. I had made a commitment not to do anything major until I had been sober for a year. This was a wise suggestion from Harold since I had been prone to make bad decisions in my past when I acted too hastily. Plus it would take at least a year to get some of the wreckage of my past straightened out.

After a year and a half—and a few months of sleeping at her and her roommate's house—on April 22, 1978, Dianne and I decided to get married. We didn't want to make it a big deal since we had both been married before, so we decided to go to the mountains and have a nice, private ceremony.

chapter 29

Dianne: Partner, Lover, and Green-Eyed Angel

A friend of mine from the local Easy Does It Club suggested that I call his sponsor, Pete Foster, who owned a farm in the Blue Ridge Mountain town of New Market, Virginia, and ask if he'd arrange a wedding ceremony for us. When I made the call, Pete said his son was a Methodist minister and would take care of everything for us.

Pete, who had been sober since 1939, was well known in the recovery community of Virginia for all the work he did with alcoholics who had nowhere else to go. When they could no longer get into the various detoxes and state hospitals, Pete would bring them out to his farm and let them dry out while milking cows and feeding chickens and doing all the other stuff that needs to be done on farms.

*

When we got there, Pete offered to be my best man and said his wife, Alma, would be Dianne's matron of honor. The ceremony was short and beautiful. The little church was half full of the sober drunks from the farm, and after the ceremony we all held hands and closed things just like they do in a recovery meeting.

I spent the next two days talking to Pete about the "old days" when he got sober, and he informed me that his sponsor was Bill Wilson, the AA cofounder. Being a career railroad man, he would visit with Bill weekly on his railroad run to New York. I was mesmerized by the stories he told and asked him if he would be my Blue Ridge Mountain sponsor, and he agreed. I would always tell the guys whom I sponsor in recovery that they have a direct link to Bill Wilson by way of Pete; they loved to hear that. We would all meet at a retreat once a year, and they had the opportunity to meet this beautiful, humble man in person.

Within six months, Dianne was pregnant with our first son, Owen. As time went on, we were able to buy our first home, and finances were starting to get good for us. Two of my greatest joys were being able to pay my child support and establish a relationship with Amy and Jason and serving as a stepfather for Dianne's daughter, Amy Marie. The two Amys became close sisters; Dianne and I would pick Amy and Jason up on weekends and give them much-deserved attention. Dianne became an excellent weekend mom to them, and I tried to be a good dad to Amy Marie.

There were a couple of testy occasions when Amy and Jason's stepfather, Chip, seemed to try to cast doubt on my newfound stability and throw a wrench into the reunification of my children with me. I assumed he still held a grudge from the adoption rejection, although he was a good stepfather at a time when I was unable to be there. I always supported him and never said a harsh word about him no matter what. It seemed his anger was a bit out of line for the situation, and I wasn't sure why. I would find out later.

chapter 30

Unqualified Executive

It was May of 1979. Business was good, and life was going great. It seemed like the more I became willing to keep showing up and doing the best I could, the more good things started coming my way. I tried to be absolutely honest in all areas of my life, and it was an interesting adventure to watch those in my life being taken back by my efforts to not embellish or put a spin on my past but to just tell it like it was. From insurance companies to the IRS, they all got the truth. Without exception, once I told people that I was an alcoholic in recovery, it was a plus rather than a liability. A good example was my new job offer.

The cable TV industry was rapidly spreading all over the country, and because the Norfolk/ Virginia Beach market was one of the most successful ones in the nation, Cox Broadcasting had decided to put it on the list to seek out a marketing manager. It was a big deal as they were hiring for a new market to be opened in Fort Wayne, Indiana. Fort Wayne seemed to have the ideal demographics to do test markets for these new channels like HBO, Cinemax, and a bunch of others. Pretty soon, all the big shots from Cox were in town. They had already been to Hartford and Atlanta, where Cox was based, but they couldn't deny the success of our market.

One of the requirements for being a marketing manager was a master's degree in business, the highly regarded MBA. As I understood it, after a couple of days of interviewing, the VP and general manager of the upcoming Fort Wayne market, John Brockman, asked the VP of our company, Roger Pierce, whom he recommended. He said that the guy he would recommend didn't have a master's degree or any other degree but that he sold the hell out of cable TV. John said, "Well, I'll talk to him." Roger told me that the Fort Wayne VP wanted to talk to me—was I interested? I said I would talk to him but reminded him that I didn't have any college education. He told me not to worry, saying that I probably wouldn't get the job anyway but that I should at least talk to him since he had recommended me. I called Harold and told him about it. He said something like, "Show up and see what happens." In other words, let things flow as they're supposed to.

As I sat in the office reminding myself to stay true to my new honesty, the door opened and John Brockman walked in. He was a big man with an obviously big ego. The first words out of his mouth were along the lines of, "The only reason I'm talking to you is Roger said you were his best marketing rep and before I go back I should talk to you. So tell me, why should I hire you when you don't have the requirements necessary to take the position and I've interviewed a number of guys who do?" I was a little taken aback by his approach but figured, *What the hell? I got nothing to lose, so let's tell him like it is.* I looked him in the eye and said, "I don't know why you should hire me, and if I was in your position, I probably wouldn't." (I thought, *If you knew about my past, you probably wouldn't even let me in your house.*) "But for some reason I seem to be pretty good at this selling stuff." He asked me to expand a bit, so I did. I didn't go into all of the mental hospitals and other details, but did tell him that I was an alcoholic in recovery and that as long as I don't drink, I seem to be pretty successful at what I do. He then asked me if I felt like I could put together a salesforce and teach them how to do what I do. I was honest and told him I felt like I could, adding that I had some ideas on how to ensure we got the maximum out of any market we went into. That was as honest as I could be. He stared at me for a bit and then stood up, shook my hand, and said he would call me tomorrow to let me know about his decision. I walked out of the room confident that I would be fine with whichever way things went.

The next morning I got a phone call, and Brockman said, "Well, I've decided to ask you to be my new marketing manager. Do you want to know why I chose you?" I said, "Sure." He said, "You are the only person I interviewed who knew what he couldn't do; everyone else spent the entire interview telling me what they could do." He then told me the company would sell my new house for me and give me the money to buy a new house in Fort Wayne. *Wow, wait until my eight-months-pregnant, working wife hears that we are moving to Fort Wayne, Indiana.*

We were only in Fort Wayne for a month before Owen was born. He was our latest pride and joy. Dianne had to get a new obstetrician at this late stage, and as fate would have it, when she went into labor her doctor was off duty so she was to deliver with a doctor she had never even met. In typical Dianne fashion, right before delivery she made the delivering doctor remove his mask so she could see his face before he went to work. I thought that was cool—always the strong woman.

My new job was going to require me give news interviews and be somewhat of a visible figure in the Fort Wayne area. I guess you could say I was becoming a bit of a celebrity. After all, I was the "fair-haired," albeit undereducated, super salesman from the East and was being closely watched by the Cox home office, as well as local media.

It was obvious that my ego was also going to have to be closely monitored. In order to stay true to my sobriety and honesty commitment, I got firmly entrenched in the local alcoholics recovery community and hooked up with a wise, old recovery mentor in Fort Wayne by the name of Jack Horner.

✳

Jack was a believer in the same spiritual approach to life as Harold and had been sober for over forty years. He also was legally blind, so I would have to go visit him every Thursday for wisdom. He wasn't hesitant to pass it out either. He was totally bald and looked almost identical to Daddy Warbucks from the Little Orphan Annie story, and, funnily enough, his wife's name was Annie. I thought, *You can't make this stuff up.* His style of sponsorship was no holds barred and no excuses allowed. It didn't matter what my complaints were, it was all part of the law of the universe and my job was to just keep showing up. Stay honest and you'll get what you need at exactly the right time. Sounds familiar.

One of the more interesting growing experiences occurred at home. It seems that Dianne was so busy breast-feeding Owen, trying to maintain a household, and get Amy off to school each day that she was oblivious to just how important I had become. Of course, I was so consumed with myself that I seldom considered her role and how tough it might be. I was soon reminded that strong women find a way to take care of themselves when in love with a self-centered egomaniac. I had mistakenly associated kindness for weakness and found out that there is a way to tell people how you feel without being cruel or accusatory.

At about six thirty one morning as Owen was enjoying his breakfast in the dark bedroom, I was getting ready to walk out the bathroom door with my standard, "Love ya, babe," when she stopped me with, "Honey, I need to share my feelings with you about something." *Uh-oh,* I thought.

"What is it, babe?" I inquired. She continued, "It really bothers me when you walk out the door and head off for the day, leaving the towels on the floor, whiskers in the sink, and the bathroom soaking wet for me to clean up after you're gone." Immediately, I went on the defensive. "My God, I've probably got to be on TV in a few minutes, and I'm trying to put these kids through college and at the same time do a job that I've never done before and not qualified to do anyway and … do it all without drinking and now I got to deal with this." Her gentle response was perhaps the most valuable communication we've ever had. "Honey, you don't have to change if you don't want to. I just needed to let you know it bothered me." Well, what am I going to do with that? She just shared how she felt, and now the ball was in my court. Of course, I changed my ways and fell more in love with this wise, strong woman.

chapter 31

What's a Marketing Plan?

O ne morning as John Brockman and I were meeting about the
upcoming strategy, he asked me when I would be able to present him with "the marketing plan." The TV interviews were
over and the celebrity stuff would now have to give way to getting
the job done. For just a moment, I was tempted to give him a date,
acting like I knew what he was talking about, and then I caught
myself and meekly offered, "Exactly what type of plan are you
looking for, and when would you like it to be complete?" He could
tell I had never done one and seemed to relish the fact that I was
suddenly caught without the education necessary to get it done.
His response was, "Just give me a date." I told him I would have a
date for him the next day. He agreed and the meeting adjourned
with him smiling a bit cockily.

I'm not sure why, but I got a rush from the challenge and never
doubted I would be able to put a marketing plan together. I instantly dropped back to what my dad had taught me years before—
find out how the best are doing it and follow their guidelines.

That afternoon found me in the local library researching
marketing plans. I started with one from the Harvard Business
School and studied it intensely. It was huge and unbelievably
wordy. The first thing obvious to me was that it included a whole

lot of information that wouldn't be relevant to us and that much of it seemed to be written just to fill space or perhaps get a passing grade. I wanted one that would tell us what we needed to know to be successful at selling cable TV.

I made what notes seemed usable and, feeling a bit homesick, went to the bookcase to find one from the University of Virginia Business School (UVA). I always felt a bit of respect for UVA since the founder, Thomas Jefferson, was one of my childhood heroes and I had read his boyhood book. I devoured the UVA plan, impressed by its conciseness and abundance of common sense. I'm sure, although swallowed up by all the nonessential details, the other plans were great, but this was my kind of plan based on its usable and practical information. I went back and told Brockman the plan would be ready in seven days unless he needed it sooner. I was on fire.

After I presented my plan to Brockman, he seemed a bit surprised by its conciseness. He had a master's degree in engineering and had probably seen a number of those Harvard-type plans. We went through each section of the plan, and each time he would question me about something, I had an answer for him, explaining how each item related to our need. I explained to him that I felt confident that I could get the marketing job done as long as we had the engineering done. I had to take a little jab at him. I knew that most of the marketing problems we encountered in Virginia had to do with various permits and cable-laying problems. Construction personnel, training, weather, unions, and materials always dictated the pace of marketing, and I had based the marketing plan on time frames he had given me. All I needed now was for him to give me the go-ahead.

After about sixty days of interacting with engineering and political leaders, we were getting close. One of the strategies in the marketing plan was to start laying the cable in the most economically deprived areas of town. Oftentimes, civic and political leaders wanted to start in the nicer parts of town, but I assured them that the poorest folks would be the best subscribers. I had experienced that in Virginia, and I had read that during the Great Depression, the movie industry had thrived. I believed that Fort Wayne Cable-Vision, our new name, would have similar results. People would pay for entertainment when they couldn't pay for anything else.

In addition, programming was getting a little attention. We were anxious to see how the new premium channels were going to do—HBO; Showtime; Cinemax; and a couple of soft-porn channels, Playboy and Rainbow. Fort Wayne is big church country, and we got a lot of heat from the local and national religious leaders. Those calls were often directed to me. I guess John Brockman didn't want to explain to Pat Robertson why we were allowing these channels in our lineup. I did my best to appease the hard-core fundamentalist leaders, to no avail of course. I suggested that they risked increasing interest in the channels by making a bigger deal of it than it really was. After all, those who wanted them would have to pay extra. Maybe the Christian Broadcasting Network would be better served talking up the positive aspects of watching CBN. I'm not sure I convinced them. After some grumbling, I was given a kickoff date.

We had a gala luncheon that included thirty-five TV sets, one for each channel; about a hundred visitors; and corporate VPs from Cox. The list also included local government and civic leaders, and it was hyped to the max. National news covered it, and just for kicks I even sent an invitation to President Carter. He explained, via his staff, that he was too busy to attend but thanked me for the invitation. After the mandatory praise was heaped on the local dignitaries, the moment was upon us. I was at the podium explaining how everything worked and finally gave the signal to engineering, which lowered the lights and started the theme from *2001: A Space Odyssey*. At the precise moment of crescendo, a button was pushed and all thirty-five TV sets came on, each showing a different channel. The place erupted, and the gala itself got a standing ovation. Cable TV was in Fort Wayne, Indiana.

chapter 32

My First Sales Team

'm sure the thought crossed my mind that this was my first opportunity to lead a team since the Marine Corps. Now that all
the administrative stuff was over, it was time to start walking
the walk. I had decided to have the sales people use street sheets
with 50 addresses on each sheet and have them kept in a loose-
leaf binder. This makes it easier for them to do their door to door
marketing and it is much less cumbersome than the fifty 3x5 index
cards used in Virginia. I also implemented a plan to require a certain percentage of sales success before a sales rep could get another
street sheet. I surmised that most sales were missed because the
prospective subscribers weren't home when the sales rep went by
and the sales rep got lazy and wouldn't go back later. We would
always leave a bright orange door hanger if we missed them, but
without knowing what the benefit was, they usually wouldn't call.

The average sales success percentage in Virginia was 43 percent; my personal success rate was about 70 percent. The percentage I planned to demand in Fort Wayne was 70 percent. I figured if
I can do it they can do it. I was determined to make this test market
a good one. With everyone knowing they would have to get 70
percent, they never missed it. A few got into the 80th percentile,
and after the first year, we had shattered every estimated success

barometer there was. This was one of my earliest examples of talented and well-trained salespeople doing what they were required to do versus what they could get away with doing. This has stayed with me for my entire business career.

As was often the case in successful sales operations, we were now surpassing the ability of construction to keep up with sales, and before long John Brockman was telling me to slow down. Perhaps my greatest frustration as a leader is having to tell my well-trained team to slow the momentum. I had dealt with this a few times in Vietnam, and this wouldn't be the last.

As the numbers in the Fort Wayne market were getting national attention, the job offers from other cable companies started flowing in from different markets. I only became interested when our market slowed down because of construction and my income started suffering drastically. I was paid based on the number of new subscribers, and with the slowdown, I felt I had to tell Brockman about the offers. He tried to sell me on loyalty and my lack of a master's degree, but I knew he was grasping at straws to try to keep me. I finally told him I was going to consider the offers if he couldn't come up with a different financial solution. I guess you could say I "shared my feelings with him," and he didn't seem to like it.

With the construction slowdown, it was possible he was going to take a hit with corporate. Construction was his responsibility.

I started going on some weekend interviews in Chicago, Arlington, and Cedar Rapids, to name a few, and with my resignation seeming imminent, I suddenly got a call from corporate in Atlanta. It seems that corporate had a new president named Bob Wright, whom I had heard was a UVA graduate. It also seemed like corporate had decided to make Virginia Beach a sort of regional training office where new MBA marketing managers could come to be trained. Would I like the job of training them? This new position would also include being the marketing manager of the Virginia Beach market, where I had started. Another interesting aspect was that the new operations manager, Steve McNulty, was also a UVA graduate. He was a brilliant fellow whom I felt had lobbied hard for me to get the job. Perhaps my marketing plan looked familiar to him and Bob. You got to love it. How could I say no? The boy was going home at last.

Once I was back in Virginia Beach, the training of a few MBAs became an education for me as well as them. Many of them were concerned with the more sophisticated principles of marketing— all good stuff they had learned in school and eagerly wanted to implement in their own markets. I have tremendous respect for anyone who puts forth the effort to get a master's degree, but without the willingness to execute and get into the trenches with the sales team to find out what the "real life" challenges are, it will be difficult to lead.

My combat experiences had taught me that in order to lead a team, you have to know where you are asking them to go and lead from the front. "Follow me" always works better than "Go get 'em, boys."

My management style was always more along the lines of systems and accountability. I theorized that the most important key to success was teaching a sales team what to do and then holding them accountable to do it. I like to refer to it as keeping score. I discovered that, with human nature being what it is, you can only "expect what you inspect." Many business leaders hesitate to follow this advice and suffer accordingly. In other words, "There's the way it ought to be, and there's the way it really is."

Once back in Virginia, where there is a large number of military families, it was obvious that we would have to implement a re-marketing program. Because of transfers and natural turnover, the entire market would turn over about every two years. In addition, we had a large number of hotels that wanted service. We established a commercial division as well as an advertising department. Once budgets were established and after laying out the plan on how I wanted things to run, I set up a batch of daily, weekly, and monthly reports and started "keeping score." This presented a new challenge for me and gave me newfound excitement.

I hired a former mayor of Norfolk, Irving Hill, as my advertising manager. Not only did he have a lot of commercial contacts, but he could turn a dollar into three. It took us about a year to get it all together. Interestingly, we ended up putting my old friend Eddie Williams in charge of commercial accounts. Things were rolling along smoothly.

Once we started getting things clicking, a common occurrence in the corporate world started unfolding. Corporate started feeling that they could get the job done for less money, and it wasn't long before they were approaching me with various offers to transfer. In order to keep paying me big bucks, they offered me positions in San Diego, Cedar Rapids, or Oklahoma City. My family life was starting to become somewhat stable, and Dianne and I had to decide if we were willing to make another move. My relationship with Amy and Jason from my first (second and third) marriage meant a lot to both of us, and we didn't want to lose that. There was a large part of me that felt like I owed them this steady connection. In addition, Amy Marie's father was only a few miles away, and I always encouraged her to keep their relationship strong. Both of our families were in Virginia Beach, and I wasn't really eager to move again. Dianne's biggest concern was finances. She would follow me anywhere as long as she felt we would be financially solvent. We also had a new son, Chad, to consider. So it would be me, Dianne, Amy Marie, Owen, and Chad who would be moving. As usual, she said the choice was mine. Hmm.

chapter 33

1982: Back in the Car Business

For some reason, I always trusted in my ability to provide for my family, and armed with this blind confidence, I reasoned that the only local job that would pay me the kind of money I was used to making would have to be in a sales management position in the automobile business. The Ford dealership I had last worked for was struggling, but I felt sure that I could turn things around for them. My program, which I would later title Gene Gorman: The Winning Edge, included two basic training programs: Action vs. Reaction Selling and Action vs. Reaction Management. They would make any business successful, I surmised, so I called and got an interview.

After putting my pitch on the dealer, I got the general manager's job. All I asked was that my management team be paid bonuses based on a percentage of the net profit. It seemed fair to me, considering they hadn't made any net profit for quite a while. He jumped at the offer.

Within sixty days we were in the black, and I was able to tell my managers they would be getting bonuses for the first time in months. At the end of the second month, as I was reviewing the financial statement with the dealer to accurately figure manager bonuses, the dealer hit me with a surprise expense that hadn't existed when we had our initial interview. All of the profit was instantly assigned to a phantom advertising account, showing we had not made any profit. When I inquired about it, the dealer informed me that he used what he wanted to use for private advertising. I reminded him that we had not agreed to that originally, and I said that my managers had done an excellent job and deserved what they earned based on the agreement. He wouldn't budge. I was furious and felt terrible for my staff, who had worked so hard at following the system I had put in place. I then informed him that I would not be able to work under these conditions and instantly resigned. It would be a long ride home, and I knew Dianne would be a bit upset.

With a wife who was a homemaker, three children at home, and two others to help support, I didn't have time to mess around. Dianne took it pretty well in spite of the fact that our lifestyle could possibly take a financial hit for a little while.

I tried to instill the same confidence in her that I had about finding a new job. In the final analysis, I believe she put blinders on and tried to stay positive. She seemed to just stay focused on being a good mom and ignored the reality of the situation.

Things took on a new urgency with my resignation and, not wanting to possibly put myself in the same situation I had left, I decided to go back into personal production and sell cars. I'm not sure why, but my confidence never wavered. I always felt like selling was a profession where each individual was really in business for themselves. If I applied the same principles I had been teaching and preaching, I could be very successful. All I had to do now was get a job.

Many of the dealers I had worked for previously were still

mindful of my past shenanigans, and I was a bit hesitant to go back to them. After doing a little research, I decided to go to the import dealers and see if I could get a job. I had worked at Checkered Flag Toyota years before and in fact had disappeared with my demo on one of my drunken escapades, leaving the car at the beach and never going back. I had made my amends to them and was well received, so I decided to approach them and see if they dared give me one more chance. Apparently, the dealer saw something in the "new me" and said yes. He was a wise businessman, and if he felt that someone could make him some money, he was willing to give it a shot. I got hired to sell Toyotas at Checkered Flag, the fifth-largest import dealer in the country, and was on my way.

*

With my immediate financial need and my previous success systems, which included teaching people how to sell and holding others accountable, I decided to apply it to myself. Checkered Flag had no real system to follow, so I set up my own daily, weekly, and monthly disciplines to achieve personal financial goals. I remembered what my dad had told me earlier about finding out how the best do things and trying to copy what they did and perhaps even do it better. Armed with this commitment to be the best I could be at selling, I devoured books written by the top sales people from various professions and attended every seminar I could. One guy in particular inspired and became somewhat of a hero to me. His name was Jackie Cooper, and he trained with humor as well as personal success stories. He would leave an impression on me that would stay with me forever. Within sixty days I was the top salesperson for Checkered Flag and stayed number one every month I was there.

Because of the system I had set up for myself, it wasn't long before most of my sales came from referrals and repeat customers. This allowed me to work off of appointments and put in a reasonable amount of time at work yet still make great money. This was important to me because my kids were starting to get involved in sports and dance recitals and I always wanted to be there to support them.

On a selfish note, one of my greatest joys was to be able to watch my kids perform. They were showing extreme talent in a variety of areas. In fact, Amy was a remarkable dancer and not only got a scholarship in fine arts at Old Dominion University for dance but also received a scholarship for her master's at Texas Christian University in Fort Worth.

Jason, my eldest son, and Chad, the youngest, both became high school all-American wrestlers. Selling afforded me the opportunity to be there for almost all of their various tournaments and performances. It would have been difficult to do that if I had been in management.

Before long, I had achieved all of the accolades I could ask for in sales and was starting to get the itch to lead a team again. I was making good money, and each month the salesman of the month would get a plaque put up on the showroom wall with his picture on it. When potential buyers walked into Checkered Flag, my mug surrounded them throughout the showroom. It became obvious to anyone who looked that I was "the man." This showing-up philosophy was powerful.

Before long, however, even I got tired of looking at me. The awards started losing some of their significance. There were numerous salesmen of the year awards, sales and marketing exec awards, awards from Toyota, and so on. Consequently, as I continued to get all of these accolades, I started noticing that most of the other salesmen would start each month with what seemed like a defeated attitude. Everyone seemed to be resigned to the fact they were all striving for second place, and for whatever reason that troubled me. I finally convinced management to take the plaques down and then let them know I was interested in the next management position that became available. I felt I could build a team and that if I got everybody to do what I was doing, we could really "light it up." It never dawned on me that most of the guys wouldn't be willing to do what I was doing.

✷

In 1986, I was asked if I wanted the new car manager's position. The present sales manager, a great guy and a good manager, had a drinking problem that interfered with his ability to lead others. It never really affected my performance because, with my personal system of sales, prospecting, and closing, I didn't need too much management help. I felt confident I could implement my Action versus Reaction personal selling system and build a team that would take us to a whole new level of success. It was really pretty simple: show up every day when you are supposed to be there and follow the "Ten Steps to Success," which was part of my system. These were the same basic selling steps I had used to achieve all the accolades I had received for the past few years.

I remembered how good it felt to see people achieve success beyond their wildest expectations. Train, motivate, and hold accountable—I had never seen it fail. I was excited.

I decided to talk to the sales manager before he left. I wanted to ask his opinion of the offer to take his position. He had been doing this a long time and was very successful before the booze got him. He knew all about my recovery, and I told him I would be there for him in case he needed to talk to someone. Then we talked business.

He informed me that I usually made more money than anyone in the company, including all the managers, just selling cars. He then told me that he had tried to get the guys to do the things I had been doing over the years but that most of them were content with just being average. He recommended I continue selling or get into training on a national level.

He knew my system and felt it was something special that could be taught all over the country. I trusted him and valued his opinion but didn't quite expect that.

After a brief tenure in management, until they could find another replacement, I went back to selling. I decided to fine tune my techniques, put my system on paper, and create workbooks I could use to train dealerships around the country. An idea had been planted in my head that I started thinking long and hard about. There was just one problem—I was terrified about getting cooped up on a plane, especially sober. I kept thinking about Jackie Cooper and thinking, I could do that—if I could just fly.

chapter 34

1987: Strange Angels— Therapists

One of the great struggles I was having was getting beyond my phobias and using the talents God had given me. When I was drinking, I had to be half drunk to get on a plane or, as previously mentioned, ride on an elevator. In other words, I couldn't stand to be in any position from which I couldn't immediately get out. By this time, it had been over ten years since I had drank. I had consistently been very active in the recovery program, and I felt like I had a good relationship and understanding of a personal God, yet I still had all of these fears, one of them being cooped up in a plane. I didn't want to be put in a position where I couldn't get out and get control. However, those comments about becoming a national trainer stuck in my head. Within a year, I had put my system together and was ready to go. All I had to do now was take action.

Patsy Crandall

It was 1987 and throughout my years of sobriety, I had done exhaustive personal inventory work while going through the twelve steps of recovery, but it was obvious that I had stopped growing and was stuck in certain areas of my life. I had accepted things as part of life when I was growing up, but now it was time to deal with the repressed anger at some of those most traumatic experiences.

My closest friend in the recovery world was Mike Burke. In fact, I guess you could say I was his mentor. He had been an active drug addict as well as an alcoholic, and as part of his recovery, he started consulting this woman named Patsy Crandall who was getting him in touch with his past so he could move on with his present. Since I was so close to Mike, I started seeing a healthy change and asked him if he thought she might be able to help me through some of these phobias that still controlled me. He said, "I don't know, but it won't hurt to go see her." I think Mike called her an experiential therapist.

I made an introductory appointment with her in which she made a freeze frame of my family as I was growing up. She wanted to know, where does everyone fit and, based on my opinion, what are each person's individual characteristics? That experience alone let me know this was going to be unlike any therapy I had ever done. In addition, she asked me to put everything on paper and describe my feelings about my parents and siblings through adjectives, good or bad. We then scheduled an intense five-day, eight-hours-a-day group workshop. Patsy suggested that I may meet who I really am for the first time. She was right.

It was by far my most powerful therapeutic experience. To be fair, every psychiatrist, psychologist, and doctor I had ever seen had helped me in some form or another, but this woman was instrumental in changing my life.

In our group, we all went back through our lives and examined every experience and relationship we could remember. Nothing was out of bounds, and everybody in the group was free to question and challenge one another's words and excuses. Each of us were given whiffle ball bats so we could vent our past rages on a vinyl bench as the other members of the group acted out various situations in which we had been injured or pissed off in our past. One beautiful girl in the group named Linda looked a lot like my mother in her younger days. After I shared that with the group, they suggested that Linda role-play my mother. She agreed and, unknown to her, played a pivotal and healing role in changing my life.

One of the major contributors to my phobias had to do with my Vietnam experiences and being trapped in situations I couldn't get out of. As luck would have it, another Vietnam veteran was in my group. We challenged each other at every turn and wouldn't allow each other to put the victim hat back on as we faced our past experiences. No one had ever heard of post-traumatic stress disorder in those days; it was all about getting out of the victim state of mind. The poor "workbench" was totally destroyed by the time the week was over. It was by far the most exhausting emotional experience in my life.

At the end of the five days, I was worn out. It seems that only after you deal with the anger and get it out can you move on and truly get out of the victim mentality.

After the workshop, Patsy's words were very simple: "Now that you are free, what are you going to do with your life?" I hesitated a moment, smiled, and then told her I was going to become a national motivational trainer who flies all over the country and teaches people about sales and sales management. She smiled and gave me a hug. That was the last I ever saw of her.

chapter 35
Facing My Phobias

By 1988, all of the kids were in school, and with the onset of my newfound goal of opening my own training company, Dianne felt it would be wise for her to go back to work. Once again, I was going to give up a very good income and start from scratch to chase another one of my dreams. She had been down this road with me before. Understandably, there would be money concerns, and Dianne felt somewhat powerless if she wasn't doing something to provide money for the household and living expenses. Since she had been out of the workforce ever since we had gotten married, I told her I would draw up a resume for her. "What a guy."

By the time I got done, you would have thought that being a homemaker qualified her to run AT&T. It might have, smart as she was. She negotiated herself a pretty lucrative deal as office manager for an oral surgeon's office and managed to get herself a four-day workweek.

My challenges were going to be a bit more difficult. I was used to making great money selling cars but would be starting from zero with my new adventure. It never crossed my mind that I couldn't be successful; my only concern was how long we could survive financially while I got it going. If I didn't book an Action versus Reaction training workshop or seminar, I didn't get paid. My only security was that I knew I could always go back to selling cars. The only other challenges were going to be driving on interstate highways and, eventually, getting on an airplane, but I'd cross that bridge when I got to it, I figured.

Booking a workshop meant getting a dealer to let me come into his dealership and train his managers and sales staff to use my ideas and techniques, which would hopefully take them to a new level of success. My reputation as a top salesman was well known in our market area, so I started trying to book myself locally. The expenses would be minimal, and I could be home each night. I held a few one- and two-day workshops for the local dealers, but then it was time to expand. This would be tougher. Each time I finished a workshop for a local dealer, he would give me a list of his dealer peer group, or what they call Twenty Groups.

A Twenty Group is usually made up of dealers from different parts of the country, outside of one another's marketing areas. These dealers meet a few times a year at a fancy resort and share ideas since there is no threat that they will compete against one another. Most of them had never heard of me, but being able to say I had just done some successful work for a member of their Twenty Group often could get me in the door, if I could get them on the phone.

I stayed on the phone constantly and designed myself a Daily Activity Report (DAR), just as I had done when selling cars. My personal commitment was to make a certain number of contacts each day using a canned pitch I had made up in order to stay on track. It was sort of like selling door to door, but this was phone to phone. Unfortunately, calling business owners is much more difficult.

Every car dealer has a built-in call-screening system designed to avoid vendors and trainers, like me, from driving them crazy. I understood that but reminded myself that it was a numbers game and that my job was to keep calling and calling and faxing and faxing, leaving the results in the hands of the "law of the universe." At least that is what Harold kept telling me.

It wasn't long before success started coming my way. During the first year, I stayed within the local states because I could drive to those locations, but before long I was being asked to come speak to the entire Twenty Groups at some of their meetings. Armed with Patsy's philosophies of "just get on the damn plane" and going with the anxiety when it hits instead of fighting it, I did it.

By this time, I had acquired a personal working faith in God and, as I would get anxious, I would just say, "You got it, God," and hang in there. There were occasions when I would get that surge of panic, but I would just stay with it, knowing it was going to pass. It always did. Before long, I was booking myself all over the United States. I even booked dealers in Hawaii and Alaska just to maximize my faith. I had been hired by General Motors to train their dealers in various parts of the country, and by way of my Rotary Club membership, I was asked to help AT&T with some of their marketing and motivational needs when the phone industry was being deregulated. My reference list was starting to look pretty impressive, and that makes it easier to get in the door.

As I got busier and busier, it became obvious that I was going to have to get a manager to take care of running my office while I was gone. I already had a secretary who was answering the phone and taking care of necessary paperwork, letters to dealers, reports, and so on, but it was time to expand. Strange things happen at just the right time.

chapter 36

Tom Wright: A Spiritual Man

O ne evening, as Dianne and I were attending Amy's college graduation party, Amy came up to me and said that her roommate's dad, Tom, wanted to meet me. The party was held at Beverly's home. Tom Wright was one of the gentlest and most mild-mannered men I had ever met. He looked like a college professor and spoke like an English gentleman. After introductions, he said he had heard I was a sales and management consultant who traveled the country doing motivational seminars. I explained that it was a little more than that but that he was close. He then said that Amy mentioned I might be looking for a business manager. I responded that I was, and he asked if he could tell me a little about his background and perhaps be considered for the position.

Once he got the green light, he was on a roll. He started by telling me that he had gone to New York City to study commercial art. He was young but married and needed income while going to school, so he took a job selling encyclopedias door to door. I was impressed right away but asked how he ended up in Virginia Beach. The story really got interesting then. Tom was a very spiritual man and was being mentored by the assistant pastor at Earl Nightingale's Church in New York City. I believe his ultimate goal was to become a minister. The pastor was friends with Pat Robertson, and Pat had asked if he knew anyone who would be qualified to be program director for the new Christian Broadcasting Network he was trying to build in Portsmouth, Virginia. Pat flew Tom there, and he was on a new mission. Commercial art was laid to rest.

The rest of the story seemed long but interesting, so I suggested that he ride with me to Gatlinburg, Tennessee. I was the guest speaker for the National Speakers Association that year, and their headquarters were in Gatlinburg. I felt the ten-hour ride would let me know if Tom and I were compatible. Once we got in the car, he finished his story.

He had been offered a much higher-paying position to help Jim and Tammy Bakker set up their new Charlotte-based Christian station and decided to move on. The rest was history. Jim Bakker started buffering himself from those on whom he used to rely for advice and soon was under investigation on criminal charges. Tom felt it best to distance himself and left. By the time he and I met, he had been selling home improvements and doing other jobs that were meaningless for a person of his experience.

It would have humbled most men, but when you're already a humble man of faith, you always know something is "around the corner." There was.

I was impressed enough by his talents that I offered him the job—one of the best business decisions I ever made. With him running the office and making follow-up calls to clients, the company took on a whole new flow. I was free to improve on the programs I was teaching, and Tom made sure nothing was overlooked. I could see why Pat and Jim had wanted him on their team.

Before long, I was on the road about twenty days a month and had frequent flier miles with so many airlines that I was almost always able to fly first class. Fortunately, I was a nondrinker, so the free drinks weren't a big deal to me. Sometimes as they were passing out the booze, I would think, *Where were you folks when I needed you?* I know that airline food gets a bad rap sometimes, but in first class, I always thought the meals were fine.

✳

Any business traveler can tell horror stories about life on the road. The divorce rate is very high for these nomadic and weary travelers. Many of those stories start off in dimly lit hotel cocktail lounges and end up in steamy hotel rooms where alcohol-fueled discussions of nagging husbands and wives become fodder for adulterous affairs. Again, being a nondrinker, I was able to avoid most of the stories. Whenever I was in a town for two or more days, I made it a point to get to a recovery meeting to be sure that the allure of the road was kept at bay.

The most challenging thing for me was to keep from eating late-night room-service meals followed by a huge dessert of the day, which always included ice cream and chocolate something or other. A meal plan like this always seemed to keep me awake half the night, and it's easy to gain weight. After learning the tricks of the road and gaining about ten pounds, I decided I had better get back in some sort of shape, so I once again started playing racquetball. I would often seek out the nearest racquetball club in the town I was working and could usually get a good workout.

chapter 37

Your Sons Are Trying to Kill Each Other

I n a committed relationship, it's easy to forget who goes through the most difficult part of the traveling experience. Business was excellent, and I was starting to make a good name for myself in the automobile industry. It seems that with most things, balance is required to maintain success—never one of my strong points.

Since I was once again appearing before droves of "worshippers" of my wisdom and taking on celebrity status, I would usually get to my room exhausted. After a hard day of motivational speaking and training salespeople from all over the country, I would immediately take a shower and then make my usual call home to check on Dianne and assure her that I loved and missed her terribly.

In the early traveling days, her response was, "Oh, yes, and I miss you too." Then it became something like, "Uh-huh, so when are you coming home?"

One of my favorite memories was a call I made from the Marriott in Phoenix. It went something like this: "Hello, darlin'. How was your day?" Her response was, "Well, I just got home, and Amy Marie was here. She had gotten a call from *your* son Chad, saying *your* eleven-year-old son Owen was trying to get in the house because *your* nine-year-old son Chad had locked him out. Chad said Owen was trying to kill him with the weed whacker and broke the door window because he wouldn't let him in." "Hmm," I grunted, and at that precise moment, the room service waiter knocked on the hotel door. "Hang on, honey. It's room service," I said. "Just put the steak over there, please." Not the right thing to say. I came back to a dial tone.

After my in-room dining, I called her back and found out the boys were fighting, as brothers do, and that Owen was teasing and jerking Chad around. Nevertheless, with all this traveling I was doing, I needed to be more involved in the boys' lives, including that of my eldest son, Jason. Even though Chip had done a good job of providing for him and Amy, It always bothered me that I never had a chance to be in his life on a day-to-day basis. I decided to make a few changes.

It became standard practice for me to take one of the boys out of school midday and do something special—movies, museums, arcades, the beach, we did it all. They loved it when the school's PA system would announce, "Chad Gorman, come to the office and bring your books."

Later, Chad and Owen told me that their friends were all jealous when they left the room. I'm sure Chad would make a wisecrack like, "Going for a fun day. See you all later." In fact, when I signed them out at the office, I would always put "Fun" in the column that asked for the reason I was picking them up. The office staff would just smile.

After a while and when the kids didn't have school, I got bold enough to take the boys with me on work trips across the country. Amy Marie was a little too old for this, so she never went. I think she had discovered boys by then. We would always make the cross-country work trips extra special. I took them one at a time, so it was always one on one and they wouldn't have to compete for

Dad's affections. We went to New Orleans, Portland, Dallas, Las Vegas, Orlando—they flew all around with Dad. In one instance, I had Chad work with me in a seminar. I made him wear a tie and had him passing out workbooks and other materials. He was glowing. Owen was always very independent and would go to the pool, walk around the lobby, or just stay in the room and order room service and watch movies for the rest of the day. He mentioned that on one trip, the bathroom even had a TV in it. *Wow*. When I got done working, we would head out for a night of fun.

One of my fondest memories was when Jason and I went to New Orleans. He had just won a big Scholastic wrestling tournament and was feeling a little cocky, so I figured I had to humble him a bit. We were staying at a fancy hotel called Le' Meridien.

As we were lying in our individual beds talking, I accused him of not being so tough and, while laughing, assured him that I could probably still turn him into a pretzel if we were ever to wrestle. Within a moment, he had jumped on my bed and put me in a headlock. We were both laughing hysterically, but I was also trying to get him under control with my famous "Grip of Kong" tickle move, all to no avail. By the time we were finished, I could barely walk; we had destroyed the bed, lamps, and pretty much the entire room; and neither of us could stop laughing. It was just one of those classic father/son moments, and it reminded me of how much I loved him and how much I had missed out on as he was growing up. I still get a bit teary eyed as I write this.

One of the decisions I made was to take temporary high-paying positions with certain local dealers who knew my reputation and with whom I had done some Action training in the past. They would often hire me to straighten out their sales teams or take them to the next level of success, and this would allow me to get off the road for a while and be more of a parent.

Working for someone else day in and day out was not my favorite thing to do; I liked the idea of working for myself. In addition, I enjoyed the traveling, teaching, and motivating, but the present times seemed to call for something else. Amy and Jason's home was in a bit of a stress mode because of some business difficulties Chip had gotten involved in. It looked like he might even have to go to jail. In addition, Dianne had paid her sole parenting dues for a long time, and now that she was working, she liked the idea of my being close. Also, I loved the fact our kids were active in sports as well as just being kids, and they needed as much support as possible.

I took a temporary job with a large local Ford dealer in Newport News, Virginia, who wanted me to "get them guys selling some cars." Newport News was about an hour from our Virginia Beach home, but the dealer was a previous client and was paying me well, so it was worth making the drive to take on the challenge. After weeding out the drug ring that permeated the used car department and getting the inventory in line, I could start hiring, firing, and training on how to effectively succeed with the Action versus Reaction Sales and Management program. In addition, we would implement our Winning Edge as a philosophy for success.

chapter 38

The Winning Edge

T he Winning Edge" was the name I chose to a certain sales philosophy I had developed while working with dealers over the
previous few years. In fact, my Action versus Reaction program
was often referred to as the Winning Edge because the logic of it
all was so profound. The reality was that some salespeople need
more help than others and some shine at different times in their
careers. Based on that belief, I wanted to find out what each individual thought he or she had the talent to do. The team's Winning
Edge was what we were looking for because it establishes what is
considered a good job by the sales staff themselves.

This was done at a sales meeting, and sales managers were
not allowed in. Everybody was asked to put a number on a piece
of paper representing what they thought they could sell with the
proper management help. They also were told to leave their names
off of the paper so they would feel safe and know there would be
no retribution for what they put down. Nationally, the Winning
Edge would result in each salesperson selling about fifteen cars
per month. Anyone who was already above that level of production
could keep doing whatever it was he or she was doing, as long as
it was ethical and honest. The focus should be on guys who were
below the Winning Edge. This kept top producers from hating

the new "hot shot" consultant the dealer had brought in and usually made them my biggest fans. You certainly don't want to go to a guy who is doing a great job and tell him, "Hey, Charlie, you're doing a good job, but here's how I want you to start doing it." That would be unfair and dumb; if what he is doing is working, why mess with it?

Once we had an average number from the existing sales team, we dropped the unrealistic 10 percent from the top and bottom that we would always get, and then we had that dealership's Winning Edge. Top producers are driven by ego and income and will generally be top producers regardless of what system is used. In addition, I found that if you raise the average or below-average producers' volume, the top guys would do an even better job because they would have to in order to remain top producers. I never saw it fail.

The next meeting was with the managers. "I have some good news. Now that we know what the sales team believes they can achieve with the proper management help, it is up to management to give them that help." In other words, after the salespeople are properly trained, management has to hold them accountable to do the things daily, weekly, and monthly that are required to reach their Winning Edge. They know they can't get there by themselves or else they would already be there. I would tell them, "In other words, you have to become an Action versus Reaction manager." Sometimes, the managers would roll their eyes at this new plan. They knew they were going to have to start working harder. As usual, I was extremely excited.

chapter 39

Tragedy Comes in Many Forms

One afternoon while at work, I got a call from Dianne telling me that Chip had just committed suicide. Although it's unclear why people do these things, some figured that the stress of his upcoming court date and prison time was just too much for him. I heard that he had started drinking heavily and apparently had crossed that line where he felt that was the only way out. Dianne said she was going over to their house to see if there was anything she could do. I told her I would leave right away and meet her there.

By the time I drove the forty-five minutes to the house, it was crowded with people. Many of them were former in-laws I hadn't seen since making amends to them for putting Beverly through those difficult years. In addition, Chip had never been a big fan of mine, so I assumed his side of the family wasn't either.

I was wrong. His family was full of good people who never really had any animosity for me. In fact, many of them seemed to respect me for the changes I had made in my life. For that, I was extremely grateful. I was there to support my children, Amy and Jason, and anyone else who might just need a hug. In her usual fashion, Dianne became somewhat of the house caretaker and was a steady force of energy and compassion throughout the next couple of days. Everyone loved her. She portrayed herself as a woman of unequaled character and strength. I was always proud of her and admired her more than ever, but now others could see her in action.

For the rest of the day, I sat in the dining room, out of the way, and just tried to be available. It was at this time that I started realizing how much I felt for Chip and Beverly's daughter, Kelly. She was a beautiful little girl and, in a strange sort of way, I felt a little responsible for her. I reasoned that, over the years, she would have to deal with a tragedy that no one should ever have to deal with. I planted in my mind that I was going to try to see her as one of my own. She and I would become somewhat close, and I always admired the way she matured over the years.

The funeral was a couple of days later, and for whatever reason, when the cars started heading to the cemetery, I was so overcome with emotion that I had to stop the car. The tragedy of it all just got to me. I was sobbing uncontrollably, and Dianne comforted me until I could regain my composure. I guess I had put on this strong face for my kids, but once we were alone I had to let it out. I'm glad Dianne was there for me.

I had completed my work in Newport News when I got a call from another local client, Tom Riddle, who was opening a new Acura dealership. He wanted me to put the Winning Edge in the new store right from the start. Tom had become a good friend, and I probably learned as much from him over the next two years as anyone else in the car business. After getting his Acura store up and running, he wanted me to put the program in his Honda Store. Interestingly enough, his biggest challenge with his Honda dealership was his service department's Customer Satisfaction Index, or

CSI. When people are upset with your company, it doesn't matter why. They will just stay away, and that affects sales as well as service. We turned things around by putting the Winning Edge in place and promoting his youngest son, who was one of the service advisors, to a position in which he would not be interacting with customers. That solved the CSI problem. His son was talented but didn't have strong people skills, a requirement for a service advisor.

Tom had been very successful but was suddenly faced with a tragedy of his own. His eldest son had just returned home to die. He had AIDS There wasn't much known about AIDS in those days, and if someone got it, it was certainly a death sentence. One morning, Tom, a strong and positive man, came into work visibly shaken. I asked him what was wrong, and he said he was sad for his son because no one would visit him for fear of contracting the disease. I guess Raymond Johnson ran through my mind, so I asked if he would like for me to go see him. He surprisingly said, "Would you mind?" I said, "I would be happy to go." I had never been up close to someone with AIDS, but my faith was strong and I just felt the need to do it.

The next morning on my way into work, I stopped and met his son. He was very frail and could barely speak. He had a wet cloth on his head, and Tom's wife, Julia, was in the room. I told their son how much his dad meant to me and how much he told everyone at work he loved him. Then I said I wanted to come see him because I knew he was special. I asked him if he had faith in the next life, and he said he did. I then touched his arm and said I hoped to see him in the next life someday. I left and tried not to question myself about why I had gone to see him. All I know is that it felt good and right.

After getting Tom Riddle's stores rolling again, I was back on the road. I had missed the travel and excitement that went with it. But now I was able to limit my trips out of town so that I could be involved in my kids' lives and assist in the parenting of teenage boys—no easy task. My fee had gone up in direct proportion to the demand for my services, and I was okay with that. That's how it works. My reputation was "out there" now, and Tom Wright was making sure that all of my previous clients were being properly treated. Life was good.

chapter 40

Gotta Love Those Kids

One of the greatest rewards of being in recovery was the opportunity to see our children grow up. Over the years, Dianne had gotten very involved in a recovery program for spouses, relatives, and friends of alcoholics, and this meant that our children were surrounded by spiritual principles in the home—at least most of the time. I was so grateful that my addictions were kept at bay by being active in recovery and weren't allowed to destroy their dreams as they prepared for the world.

Amy Gee, my and Beverly's daughter, had gone on to college by now, and Amy Marie got married right out of high school, so they had become busy with their own lives.

One of my proudest moments was when Amy Marie came to Dianne and informed her that she and Brian, her boyfriend, wanted to talk to us one evening. Dianne already had an idea that she was going to say she was pregnant; I guess women know about these things because of some secret connection they have with their daughters. I had no clue.

When Amy Marie and Brian sat down, Brian started by telling us that they were going to have a baby and that they had decided to get married. Brian had come from a very fundamental religious family, and I felt that maybe they had suggested that getting married was the "right thing" to do. After listening to them tell their story, I asked Brian why he wanted to get married. He stumbled a bit and said, "Because I think I can make her happy." I somewhat aggressively responded that I hoped he wanted to marry her because he loves her and that I hoped she already was happy. I then continued a bit more gently. "Why would you want to marry her if she isn't happy? Her job is to make herself happy, and yours is to make yourself happy. If you're happier together that's great, but the baby will be loved and cared for whether you are married or not."

I'm not sure why I said that. Perhaps I wanted to remind them or make them aware that a healthy relationship required each person to take care of his or her own needs and not rely on the other person for happiness. Maybe I was trying to protect Amy by taking the pressure off of both of them so they could start life on the right track. Obviously, they already had the romance part down. Anyway, we gave them both hugs and said we would support them in whatever they chose to do.

They decided to go ahead and get married, and it made me very proud that Amy Marie chose to attend her graduation with her class, eight months pregnant, smiling and wearing a bulging graduation gown.

My sons Jason and Chad had gotten into high school and junior high wrestling and were starting to experience a lot of success. In fact, Jason went through his freshman year without being scored on, a remarkable accomplishment. He would go on to be a High School All-American as a sophomore at the National High School Championships in Lehigh, Pa. He was already getting looks from various colleges around the country and was showing signs of being somewhat of a "phenom." Unfortunately, he was involved in a serious car accident right before his junior year in which his foot was almost severed, and he lost the ability to compete at the high level necessary to move on in wrestling. Being somewhat disheartened, he quit school after a couple years of college and moved back and forth from California to Colorado to continue pursuing his other passions, surfing and snowboarding.

Owen had no real interest in team sports; he seemed to be more into the individual, speed-associated sports like BMX racing and surfing. He was always the most independent of the boys. He wanted to know how things ran and would take anything apart just to find out. At a very young age, he was extremely organized and would have all his shoes lined up and shirts hanging in a certain order so that it was easy to pick what he wanted. I thought that was rather unusual for a thirteen-year-old boy.

I often wondered where his future would lie. I always admired the way he handled his brothers' getting all the attention that came from being star athletes. Being somewhat concerned, I told him one day, "You know, son, we all shine at different times in our lives." He responded, "I know, Pop. It's okay. I'm proud of them." I started thinking that, with his being independent and having these early organizational skills, he would probably be going into business for himself someday. That would eventually come about in a much unexpected way, and he would have his time to really shine.

And then there was Chad, the baby in the family and by far the most outgoing in personality. At eleven years old, Chad would try anything from bungee jumping to parasailing (with Dianne, I might add), and he became the family entertainer. As an elementary school student, he became a Stephen King fan and before long, despite the raised eyebrows of his teachers, he was doing book reports on Stephen King novels. In fact, he was on the waiting list at the local bookstore for each newest novel before it came out. He was always popular at school, and because of his sense of humor everybody wanted to be around him. My constant advice to him was to use good judgment and not let his friends decide his future. He was an excellent student and athlete, and there were early signs that he was going to do something special with his life. I just wanted to make sure it was something positive.

chapter 41

1994: Our Great Florida Adventure

O ne of my largest clients was in a small southwest Florida town called Punta Gorda, part of Charlotte County. *Punta Gorda* is Spanish for "fat point." History tells us that it was visited by Ponce de Leon, of whom there is a statue erected at one of the coastal parks. All I knew was that it was one of the most beautiful places in the world, and for about eight months out of the year, the weather made it seem like heaven. During the other four months, people just sort of hang on through the heat and possible hurricanes or go north. Those who leave are referred to as snow birds. They usually start flocking in around October and flying back north in late April or May.

Most of the local economy is directly affected by the season change. Palm Automotive was the largest car dealer in the county and perhaps in the entire southwest part of Florida. They were what's commonly referred to as a megadealer; in other words, they had multiple new car franchises at one location. They had been on the Winning Edge program for over a year, and we had increased their production and profit by about 30 percent. This would translate into millions of dollars, and understandably they were one of my biggest fans.

Around March of 1994, the management at Palm was looking for ways to expand their dealerships. The idea was to create a mall concept that would take up two full blocks on the main street in the heart of Punta Gorda. They had looked within the organization for someone to be the general sales manager (GSM) but felt it would be best to go outside the organization and try to entice me to take the position. The present GSM was a good guy, but I assumed he was being eased out of the position because they felt he might not be the guy for the future. This would not be a consulting contract; it would be a job—albeit a potentially very well-paying job. I thought, *With the strides they've made using the Winning Edge and with the manager easing out, if I was there every day, we could really light it up.*

When I got the offer, my first reaction was negative. I had some apprehension about giving up my business and going back to work for someone else. I had been down this road before. I started weighing the pros and cons and used the formula given to me by my mentor, Harold, regarding major decisions. He suggested removing fear and guilt from all decisions and just listing the real pluses and minuses.

I also considered Dianne's words from years before: "If I ever moved anywhere from Virginia Beach, it would only be to Florida." I considered the uprooting of the boys in their young teenage years and how it might affect them. I considered the giving up of my freedom and how much that meant to me. Then Dianne and I talked.

She was also apprehensive about the change. We had gotten to a point at which we were both relatively stable, and Owen and Chad were doing well in school and their respective sports—Owen's BMX and surfing and Chad's soccer and wrestling. As I said, life was good but I was still traveling more than either of us wanted and this seemed like an ideal opportunity and it was in beautiful South Florida. I told Mickey McHale, the CEO, that

I would let him know. He then called me back and said, "The Helphenstines, who are the owners and founded the company, would like to invite you and Dianne to spend a week at their condo in Boca Grande. It will be a good place for you to think about it."

It isn't an exaggeration to proclaim Boca Grande, a community on Gasparilla Island, as one of the most beautiful places in the world. The beaches are pristine white and the sand as soft as talcum powder—a perfect place to think about something. It's also famous for its tarpon fishing, and both President Bushes would come each year to fish and enjoy the relaxing atmosphere. We figured, what the heck? Let's at least take a vacation if nothing else, and then we can look around the community and see what we think.

By this time, Dianne and I were both golfers, and after playing at a few fancy South Florida courses and loving the beach, we had made our decision. Then it was time to talk money and tell the kids.

Mickey McHale was good with expenses but didn't seem to have very good people skills, and I got the feeling he didn't really care. He would be the first to say, "That's why I've got you." I knew this going into the negotiations and tried to prepare myself. The first thing I said was, "In order for me to make this commitment to sell my consulting business, I would need some sort of contract with Palm." By this time, I had my entire training program on video and sold them across the country, and they were a major source of income for me. I had also, upon occasion, hired a couple of fellows from different parts of the country to work with me. I called them my associates. In fact, the legal name of my corporation was and still is Gene Gorman and Associates Inc. One of those associates, Paul Nalle, was eager to buy the rights to my videos and client list if I ever decided to sell.

Contracts were not very common in the car business in those days, and I knew this. In fact I had never signed anything more than a one-visit contract, payable after the workshop was done, with any of my Winning Edge clients. I used to tell dealers, "If what I'm teaching your sales team isn't making you more money instantly, you shouldn't have me back." They really liked that idea, and I did too. Mickey knew this from our past experience and instantly became defensive. He said, "Christ, Gorman, if you can't trust me by now, maybe we need to back away from this."

I felt I had him where I wanted him, so I said, "Rather than back away, how about you draw me up a pay plan exactly like the guy who I'm replacing, and if I do a better job, I'll make more money than him, and if I do a worse job, you can fire me?" He liked that idea and agreed to it immediately. The only question I asked was, "Are you sure you want to pay me on gross profit and not net?" He was quick to respond, "You make the gross, Gorman, and I'll take care of the expenses." That sounded good to me. The deal was set; now to break the news to the kids. *This ought to be fun.*

The first thing we did before flying home to tell the kids was check out the highest-rated schools in the area and find out which one had the best wrestling program. I then went to the gym and talked to the wrestling coaches to let them know there was a budding superstar named Chad Gorman heading their way. They laughed and said, "Bring him on down. We can use him." We then found out there was a world-class BMX track in Punta Gorda, as well as a mall only a few miles away. I broke out the video recorder and did my version of Steven Spielberg, taping the track as well as the high school and middle school where the boys would be attending. We also filmed the mall, movie theater, parks, and anything else we thought might help with the sales job I would have to put on the kids. I was going to have to try and convince a twelve- and a fourteen-year-old that moving to this primarily retired-person town was going to be a positive experience for them. *This may require my best sales job ever.*

✳

A couple of nights later, as we got our courage up, Dianne and I sat down with Owen and Chad and said, "We have some news for you." I said, "I'm going to be taking a job in Florida, and we feel like it is going to be good for everybody." Chad interrupted and asked, "So does that mean you're going to be coming home on weekends?" The moment of truth was upon us. I broke out my video camera and started running the tape. They sat silently as I informed them that we would all be moving and started showing them some of the highlights of their new home-to-be. They didn't seem impressed. I couldn't blame them. It's hard to beat Virginia Beach when you are a young person, and it's really hard to leave all your friends. I tried to sell it as an adventure and reassured them that we would make life good for them. I told them that their mom wouldn't be working anymore, we'd be living on the water, we'd get a boat, blah, blah, blah. In the end, they took it as well as could be expected, and after a few days, they did their best to get excited.

The moving vans arrived right after the kids got out of school in the middle of June 1994. I had negotiated a buyer for my business, and in case things didn't work out financially as quickly as I anticipated, I held mutual rights to the sales of my video and audio tapes. Dianne sold or gave away most of our beautiful Queen Anne furniture and eagerly awaited the tropical-theme shopping sprees for our new house once we arrived in Punta Gorda.

✳

I knew it would be important to get hooked up with an alcoholic recovery group as soon as I arrived, lest I start thinking I was a big shot now that I had this high-paying job. I remembered clearly how easy it was for me to feel like I was the newly arrived savior from my past experience in Fort Wayne. In a short period of time, I was firmly entrenched in the local community of other alcoholics and drug addicts who were on the same sober path I was on.

Our home was a modest yet comfortable one situated on a large canal that led to the Peace River, which would quickly take boaters to the Gulf of Mexico. All of our neighbors had huge boats that could easily motor or sail to anywhere in the world, and some of them did during the summer months. *Forbes Magazine* rated Punta Gorda the best small town in America that year; it would be hard to find a better place to live. The climate was ideal for eight months out of the year, and the entire town was surrounded by water and golf courses—perfect for retired folks but not so interesting for teenage boys. It would be important to get Owen and Chad involved in something as soon as possible. Idle minds are not good for young people, and it would be late August before school started.

My new position wouldn't start until July 1, so I had a couple of weeks to honor my commitment to the boys to get a boat. Since none of us had any boating experience, I made a deal with Owen: if he and his mom would take a local Coast Guard Auxiliary course and complete it, I would buy a boat. Chad was too young to take the course and Dianne was not really interested in learning how to run a boat, but she agreed. Three weeks later, after their successful graduation, we bought a little eighteen-foot motorboat. You would have thought we had purchased *a luxury liner.*

We proudly sailed the harbor that first day and promptly ran aground about three times until we figured out how to avoid some of the very shallow waters of the Peace River. As we sat idle, we were dwarfed by the neighbors' passing monster boats, and they raised their eyebrows with a sad look of pity for us "poor" beginners.

Owen immediately fell in love with the boat, and within a year we had upgraded to a bigger and fancier one. The idea of having control of something with a motor that goes fast intrigued him. To this day, he loves the water and, as an adult, owns two boats of his own. In fact, he became a competition fisherman with some outfit called the Flatmasters. Somewhere along the way he decided he wanted to scuba dive. I agreed, but first we insisted that he take a certification course. The BMX bike thing was quickly shelved for the adventures of water sports and real motorcycles. When he turned sixteen, he got a job while going to school and took on Suzuki motorcycle racing, much to the concern of his mother and me. Anyway, once we got that first boat, he quickly became content. Now for Chad.

Chad really had no interest in boats. His sports had been soccer and wrestling in Virginia Beach, and since wrestling was only available in school, we immediately found out where the local community soccer teams practiced. I reasoned that his personality and energy required him to get active in something positive as soon as possible. I thought back to my own youth and remembered some of the negative things I did just because "it seemed like a good idea at the time." *Get that boy busy quick.*

It was obviously very important to Chad to make a statement through his athletic ability right away. His personality would always carry him socially, but when you're the new kid in town, performance speaks louder than wit.

He had always been a good athlete, but now he was really starting to shine. By the time he had been practicing with the local team for a few weeks, he was placed on the select team, which is made up of kids who seem to have the most talent and drive to win. Within a month, he had been chosen as a member of the under-thirteen (U-13) United States team to go the Junior Olympics in Belgium. He was now content and adjusted quickly to his new friends as well as competition.

Because she was no longer working outside of the home, Dianne had the ability to take him wherever he needed to go.

Sometimes he had to go a hundred miles to practice for the US team, but she was always there with that beautiful can-do spirit of hers.

In fact, when the team was looking for adult volunteers to go to Belgium as chaperones on that big fancy 747, she wanted badly to go. Unfortunately, Chad wanted to be on his own with just the team, so she honored his wishes. I did have to do a little consoling; after all, he was her "baby." As a side note, the US won the tournament, and Chad scored the winning goal in a final game shootout. Life was going good for the boys. Now, about that job.

chapter 42

Exceeding Expectations

One of the first things I had to do at Palm Automotive was create an atmosphere of harmony even though three of the managers on my staff felt like they should have been the ones who got my job. Their attitudes, as well as the eye-rolling camaraderie with their sales staffs when in my presence, made it apparent that I was going to have to start with a firm line of who was in charge without sabotaging their effectiveness. I had learned that it is more important that people know where you stand than *like* where you stand. I decided to do a one-on-one meeting with each of them.

I offered a bit of compassion for all of the change taking place followed by assurance that negativity would not be tolerated. I added that if any of them felt like they couldn't abide by these guidelines, I understood and would understand their leaving. But, if they chose to stay, it would have to be on my terms. Achieving our goals must be done with leaders who were positive and enthusiastic. I gave them all forty-eight hours to think about it; they all chose to stay. Now my job was to earn their respect.

Our sales team was made up of twenty-five to thirty salespeople, and the team was averaging about 280 cars per month. My personal goal was to take the organization to five hundred sales per month and increase the per-sale profit. My research had shown that we were losing a great deal of business to the other franchise dealers of the same name brand in Fort Myers and Venice, twenty-two miles away in each direction, although our county was one of the fastest growing in the country and was the fastest-growing retirement county in the United States.

My experience had shown me that in order to reach five hundred sales per month, we were going to need fifty salespeople on staff and five constantly in training—not an easy task in little old Punta Gorda. Generally, ten sales per salesperson was the average, and salesperson turnover would be about 10 percent per month. That's just the nature of the business, but I knew turnover would decrease as their incomes went up. At our first sales meeting, I announced to the entire organization my plans to double the sales staff, and the grumbling was unanimous. I noticed some of the sales managers looking around the room and grinning with what seemed like a "how do you like ol' Clean Gene now?" look. They were all privy to my days at Auto World, which I had talked about as part of my training on how *not* to do things. I also shared the nicknames of the guys, and they always got a big kick out of that. In fact, many of them would mimic Docky-Wocky and Fast Louie during training breaks. It was now time to do one-on-one meetings with the salespeople.

I explained to each one of them what was going to be required daily, weekly, and monthly. Furthermore, I told them that I understood if they couldn't go along with it but that if they chose to stay and work harder, they would all make more money. I also gave them two weeks to think about it, unless their attitudes became negative and then I would make the decision for them. Since I had been working with Palm as a consultant for some time, they knew the basics of the Winning Edge program. They just didn't realize the accountability that was going to be demanded of them with me on location every day. I knew that was going to make some of them nervous. It also made me a bit nervous. After two weeks, they all stayed. Hallelujah!

Mickey McHale pretty much let me do my thing with the sales team, and that was a good thing. Once a week, we would have a meeting with the comptroller and general service manager to review inventory and talk about certain decisions that needed to be made as a management team, but sales and finance were my babies. Within three months, we were on target to reach our goal. I had to change the finance managers' bonus plan a bit because they were being paid bonuses based on a very average job. All I did was research the average success numbers from all of the dealers in Florida and required our finance managers to be in the top 10 percent to receive any bonuses. They never missed their bonus, made more money, and took greater pride in a job well done. Amazing—all we had to do was raise the bar and they cleared it. Long before, I had learned that mediocrity can become the norm if you let it. The comfort zone was alive and well.

As part of my daily routine, I made it a point to walk the entire two blocks twice a day, physically shaking hands or patting everyone on the back. This would take about an hour and a half each trip, but with fifteen different franchises, it was the most important thing I could do. I surmised that my most important role was to keep a positive attitude circulating throughout the entire organization. The system was in place, and my daily and weekly reports would constantly tell me what was working and what needed attention. Any reprimanding was to be done in private. I knew I could only expect what I inspected, so everyone knew that at any moment, the boss might be walking in the door. It was working and working very well.

By month four, we were starting to roll. We had our annual car show in the fall, and with the early return of some of the snow birds, I felt like this could be our five hundred month. The tension rose as we moved closer and closer, and the vibes in the whole organization were rising. Five hundred cars in little Punta Gorda would mean we had finally started getting back the business we had been losing to the surrounding markets and making a statement as the new "big dog" in southwest Florida. In the car business, there is an old saying that the best time to sell a car is right after you've sold one. You're pumped up, you feel invincible, and confidence is oozing out of every pore in your body. Multiply that by forty-five to fifty salespeople, and you can imagine the energy. I guess it's like the physics law that a body in motion tends to stay in motion and a body at rest tends to stay at rest. Well, we had a bunch of bodies in motion.

I think the final tally was over 550. Every one of my managers congratulated me, as I did them, and the salespeople were now unanimous in their belief that we were the best and that they really could do more than they ever believed they could. That was where my joy came from. Damn, I felt good.

Mickey didn't seem to share in the enthusiasm of everyone else in the company about our record-breaking numbers. I wasn't sure why but had my suspicions. I was to find out at the next management meeting. It seems that all of the managers had hit all of the numbers to earn the bonuses available to them and were on track to do it again now that they knew they could do it and the Winning Edge was in full bloom. This meant that the company made more gross profit than it had ever made. Of course, that might mean that when Mickey went to the next dealer Twenty Group meeting, he would have to explain why his management and sales commission percentages were so high. Mickey was used to being the expense-controlling king, and now he might have to explain to his peers how it got out of control. There's that damn ego again. The cardinal sin for dealers is to think they can get the job done for less once they have started making good money. Consequently they often then self-destruct.

It seemed that Mickey's solution was going to be simple: take a 10 percent surcharge out of each manager's pay. When he mentioned this to me, I was a bit taken aback. "How am I going to go to the managers who have done the best job ever and congratulate them with, 'You've done a hell of a job and for your reward we're going to cut your pay'?" I asked.

The other managers in the meeting offered no help; hell, all of my managers were making more money than they were. Mickey responded, "Don't worry, Gorman. I'm not surcharging your pay." I said, "If you surcharge theirs, you've got to surcharge mine." I walked out of the office shaking my head and went to break the news to my managers.

I was so angry at the changing of the deal that I almost quit. I had been down similar roads before. When I broke the news to the guys, they shrugged and said it was typical. I assured them that we were all going to be sharing in the surcharge. I did my best to keep them pumped up and going full steam ahead but knew it would take a while for them to recover.

When I got home, I shared the news with Dianne, and she encouraged me to shake it off and not do anything impulsively. "We can't let this disrupt our home. My God, you're still making 50 percent more money than you've ever made in your life." I said, "Yeah, but I can't trust that son of a bitch, and I don't know if I can work for someone I can't trust." Her logical thinking, of course, was, *Here we are living in Florida, boys are doing great in school, and you're going to quit your job?* I saw the fear in her eyes and assured her I would stay put and see how things looked in ninety days.

Thank God that Harold was only a phone call away. I could always bounce my thoughts on these types of situations off of him, and he would always go back to the simple philosophy of "show up and trust God."

The next day, I went back to work with new resolve, committed to controlling what I can control and not worrying about things I can't. That was the message I presented to my managers, and they seemed to agree. I proposed that we take the surcharge, accept it, and "blow the lid off the goals," regardless of the new surcharge. They regained their enthusiasm, and before long we were back to clicking along in record fashion.

chapter 43

Florida Becomes Home

B y this time Dianne had turned our home into a tropical show-case. Her touch in decorating was something I had never really appreciated until she had a new project and I was home every night to see it happen. She had also made new friends and seemed to enjoy her return to being a stay-at-home mom.

Owen was fifteen, doing well in school, and starting to show signs of a little business acumen. One day while visiting me at work, he ran into the guy who did the pinstriping on our cars, in addition to the door-edge guards and little detailing jobs around the dealership. The next thing I knew, Owen had been hired by that guy and was asking me if it would be okay for him to start working after school to make himself some extra cash.

I smiled and started beaming a bit with "Dad pride." "Of course," I answered, and that was that. The next thing I knew, he had written out a small business plan and was now an entre-preneur. I thought, *I guess my intuition about him was right.* The following year, he was getting out of school early on a learn-and-work program, and his teachers, I learned later, were amazed at his work ethic.

Chad had just started middle school and, as usual, was making all A's. Everybody loved him. Sadly, soccer and wrestling were not offered in the middle schools, but once the high school wrestling coaches found out about his elementary school wrestling prowess in Virginia Beach, they talked him and a few of the other middle school kids into coming over to the high school to work out with the team.

Chad had been wrestling since he was seven. I used to take him all over the southeastern United States to wrestle other kids his age and compete against the best youngsters in the country. We would ride for hundreds of miles listening to the Carpenters, my favorite group, sing their sad songs. Chad later told me that his friends wondered how he knew the words to all of these oldie songs. Anyway, soccer was out, and wrestling was in. In fact, he started for the varsity team for the next four years, and they won the state championship in his freshman year. A few years later, as previously mentioned, Chad went on to become an All-American and the entire team was put into the high school hall of fame. Dianne and I were thrilled. I guess you could say Chad had settled in pretty well to his Florida community.

By now the entire sales team had accepted the new terms, and we continued to grow and grow as a company. Over the next six months, volume and profit continued to increase. In fact, my annual personal income became very substantial. Now, it's true that we were all working our fannies off, but I was making a lot of money for sleepy ol' Punta Gorda, Florida. Even I was amazed at how well the Winning Edge program was working.

It was August 1995 when Mickey called me into his office privately and informed me that he was going to have to adjust everyone's pay again. I then reminded him that everybody's earnings were based on their pay plans and that my earnings were based on the original deal we had made a year earlier. In addition I felt I needed to remind him that the company was more profitable now than it had ever been. He wasn't impressed and then went on to inform me that he was going to have to take my company car away from me and make me pay my own insurance. I was totally blown away.

Almost every car dealer of Palm's size in the industry provided a demo for their general sales manager, and many provided one for their wives as well. In addition, it would be a bit embarrassing. All of the other salespeople and managers know a car is automatic for a GSM. It felt like a slap in the face, and I just didn't understand the business logic. I was disappointed. I shook my head and walked out the door. Then I got angry. "Fucking egomaniac," I whispered to myself.

chapter 44

Time for a Ninety-Day Sit-Down

E arly on in our marriage and after a few futile shouting matches, Dianne and I made a commitment regarding disagreements. Whenever we were at odds with each other about something, we would each take a separate car, meet at a quiet public restaurant with a list of the things that bothered us about the other person, and discuss them. We wouldn't debate who was right or wrong; we just shared what was bothering us. Some of the issues seemed big at the time, but instead of just breaking up, we agreed to put the list aside for ninety days and meet again to see if the issues had been resolved. The other person could either change or accept what was on the list.

Over thirty-six years, we've probably had five of these "sit downs." We never had to go back and rehash the previous issues, and most of the time we had either changed or forgotten what was on the list. The next six months were going to present the relationship with our biggest challenge yet.

After leaving Mickey's office, I wandered around in a state of shock. I just didn't understand why this guy would jeopardize the company's success with this type of action. I called Harold.

He suggested that maybe he was trying to ease me out or maybe had miscalculated how successful I could make the company and couldn't handle it. Then again, maybe God had other plans for me. He suggested that I pray for wisdom to do what was best for everyone, including Mickey, and then reassured me that God was going to take care of me no matter which way I decided to go. Harold was easy; now I had to tell Dianne what I was thinking.

When I got home that night, Dianne could see on my face that I was troubled. Finally I told her what had gone on that day. As usual, she looked for the pony in the pile of horse manure and said, "Aren't we lucky we have the money to buy a car?" She saw the dollar-and-sense logic of it all, but deep in her heart she knew this was a potential deal breaker. I told her I just didn't know if I could work for Mickey anymore. She cried, and I held her and said not to worry. I told her, "Whatever I do, we'll be okay." It was obvious that the situation was scaring the hell out of her; she got a bit feisty and said, "We are not moving back to Virginia." I tried to reassure her and told her I hadn't decided what I was going to do yet but that we wouldn't be moving. Understandably her primary concern was uprooting the boys, while saying nothing about the financial concerns she must have had.

Things were testy around our house for a while, and it became clear that Dianne was settling into a depression. She was filled with that feeling of impending doom, and I was concerned about her. In the final analysis, I agreed to buy a car and try to hang on for ninety more days to see how I felt, but deep down I knew I was going to have a hard time staying and working with Mickey.

✱

With the help of my recovery friends and Harold's spiritual perspective on things, I was able to keep my attitude upbeat, and business kept rolling along at record levels. Every day since I first got sober, I've started my day with a prayer to be moved to do what

God's will is for me. With my continued day-to-day interaction with Mickey, it became more and more difficult to go to work and look him in the eye. By November of 1995, I had decided that I was going to resign and go back on the road. I didn't tell Dianne right away. I figured I would wait until the time was upon us. This would be very difficult for our family, but after a lot of prayer I felt like I was being drawn to take some sort of action.

It was pretty standard for the managers to get a substantial bonus on the fifteenth of December, and my year-end bonus was expected to be huge. In spite of the fact that it had been about four months since the last pay-plan adjustment and company car loss, I felt December first would be a good time to resign. My friends would later tell me I was crazy, but I was still very angry and wanted Mickey to know that I was not going to be held hostage by a Christmas bonus; this was really about the trust I had lost for him. My timing and words were such that everyone was caught by surprise. After all, things were good and you would think the blow to my ego would have long been forgotten—but it hadn't.

I walked into Mickey's office when he was alone and was greeted by the standard, "Hello, Gene O." I sat down and without any hesitation said, "I've decided to resign and thought I would tell you before bonus time so you can give me or not give me whatever you feel is fair for the job I've done."

The shock on his face was obvious, and his next words were, "Have you talked this over with Dianne?" I assured him that we had discussed this at great length but that this was my decision and no one else's. I then said that no one else knew and that I would keep it quiet until he wanted to announce it. He asked if I had given it a lot of thought, and I said, "I've been thinking about this for quite some time." I stood up and told him I would go on with business as usual until he decided how he wanted to handle the announcement. I walked out the door. When I turned the corner, I was overwhelmed with gratitude and a resounding sense of self-esteem. I think I was even smiling. God, I felt free.

A couple of days later, Mickey called me into his office and said the announcement would take place at the sales meeting on December 15. I mentioned it to no one until the morning of the fifteenth. After the meeting, no explanation was necessary from me, and no one asked. They all understood, and most of them were probably amazed that I had stayed on as long as I did.

My last order of business and one of my most gratifying meetings with Mickey was the one in which I recommended my replacement. Mickey called me into his office, where we were joined by the comptroller and the general service manager. I sat down and they asked me if I thought anyone who was presently with the company would be able to do my job. Most of the guys who had wanted my job previously were being considered, but I suggested Tonya Blair, the female used car manager who wasn't even on their list. There was some discussion about her weight and the company image. I assured them that, heavy or not, she was still very neat, extremely organized, and the most loyal and knowledgeable person they had. They fought me on this image thing for some time but finally relented, and Tonya is still the general sales manager as of this writing, some eighteen years later. By the twenty-fifth of December 1995, I was gone.

It was no surprise to me that Mickey was also gone shortly after I left, and the company went back to doing things the way they had been doing them before my arrival. Interestingly enough, the comptroller and general service manager were gone shortly thereafter as well. Now what was I going to do?

When I got home that night, Dianne was barely speaking to me. I had told her the previous day what my plan was, and even though she didn't agree with me, I felt I needed to let her know before anyone else. I assured her that something good was going to come up, and the worst-case scenario was that I would have to go back on the road and teach my sales and management program. For some reason, my faith was strong.

I never doubted my success capabilities. My faith in God was strong, and even though I might be gone three or four nights a week, I felt we would be able to maintain our present lifestyle. I vowed I would never put myself into a position where someone else could decide my fate again. Dianne's biggest concern was sharing in the raising of two teenage boys—certainly an understandable one.

chapter 45

The Life and Times of a Used Car Dealer

A s I was driving home the day of my departure, heading toward Fort Myers to attend one of my recovery group meetings, I noticed a guy putting up a "For Sale or Lease" sign on a deserted lot about a half mile south of Palm Automotive. Just the day before, it had been a recreational vehicle sales and service business. I turned in sharply, introduced myself to a guy named John, and asked him how much he was asking for the place. He told me he worked for the owner but was charged with getting it ready for sale. The buy figure seemed reasonable, but I couldn't commit to buying because I didn't have a job, so I said, "Do you think he would lease it with a first right of refusal to buy in a year?" He said the owner lived in Naples and preferred to sell it but would lease it for the right price.

After telling me the monthly lease price, I suggested it was a bit high but said I was willing to take a look at it. On and off throughout my automotive career, as is the case with most car salespeople, I had dreamed of owning my own little dealership and had even drawn up a business plan a couple of years earlier.

There were two buildings and a tall garage on the lot. One

building was a sales office, and the other was a parts department. Surprisingly, all of the equipment, furniture, phones, fax machines, and computers were still exactly where the previous tenant had left them. In fact, all of the used parts, refrigerators, and toilets were still on site. By law, any of those items had to go to a dump, and the owner would have to pay extra to dump the items that used chemicals as part of their operation. Damn, I never knew toilets broke down so much in RVs. There must have been thirty to forty of them on site. The previous tenant had gone broke, left everything, and headed out of town.

My mind and my adrenaline started racing. The rent fit my business plan formula, and the location was perfect. It was only two miles from my house and near the kids' schools. I thought, *This place is ready to do business right now. All I need to do is clean it up, get a license, buy some cars, and get rocking.* Realizing John was probably anxious to get the deal done quickly so he wouldn't have to unload the mess that had been left, I blurted, "I'll tell you what I'll do. If your owner will let me have the place just as it is right now, equipment and everything, and give me first right of refusal to buy within a year, I'll give you one month's rent and an equal security deposit right now, and you won't have to worry about anything." His eyes got big, and he said he would get back to me in a couple of hours. That's how long it would take to get to Naples and talk to the owner.

I didn't dare call Dianne yet but immediately headed out to look at what kind of cars the other used car dealers were carrying and started making notes. I already had my plan; now all I had to do was my research and market analysis and then get the ball rolling. I waited impatiently for the call. As promised, John called me and excitedly said the owner would do the deal and would be glad to sell me the equipment with a separate contract at a very reasonable price. I cautiously informed him that if that was the case, I would just get my own equipment and furniture and, if we could adjust the lease price down a bit, we would have a deal. I reminded him that he was going to have to unload all this equipment, clean the place up, and pay the chemical item disposal fees. He said, "Let me work on him a bit." Within another hour, he said he was on his way with a lease and to pick up the rent and deposit. Wow, I was almost a car dealer. Now to tell Dianne.

The approach I used with Dianne was to try to get her as excited as I was about this newest adventure. She did her best to be positive but was still smarting from the resignation and financial fear. I told her that once I got my license, I would be able to stay home and wouldn't have to travel. Until then, I would have to go back on the road doing workshops, but it would be temporary. She tried to believe me but knew how much I loved to train and motivate; I would have to prove to her that I was sincere. I understood that.

✱

Over the course of the next few weeks, I was busy going to dealer school and submitting applications for all of the various licenses, zoning permits, bonds, and so on to be a car dealer. An exhaustive time period was to follow, and it took about three months before I was able to start selling cars. Dianne became very supportive in that time frame, and I explained to her that I needed her level-headedness to do my marketing research. Armed with the facts, I had already signed the lease; she joined me on trips to visit other dealers outside of our market area to get some tips on how to be successful. I had talked to some of my Palm suppliers, who were glad to have me as a new client, and they referred me to certain successful dealers around the state to learn from. I discovered that all I had to do was reassure them I would be opening outside of their market area and tell them that so-and-so said they were excellent dealers and would be good people for me to learn from. Once flattered, they usually told me everything. Successful people are never afraid to share ideas because they know most people aren't willing to do what it takes to be successful. We both learned a lot on these trips.

Now all I needed was to get some money to buy some cars. I had excellent credit by this time and felt sure that with the great business plan I had drawn up, any bank would love to have me as a client. I even wrote up an investor letter to make sure they would be confident I knew what I was doing. Furthermore, this was a unique opportunity for them to get in on the ground floor of this new enterprise. It may have been the finest proposal I have ever done.

It included my high-powered resume (minus the mental institutions and detoxes) and a complete marketing plan. As usual, my enthusiasm far exceeded reality. I was turned down by everybody. All of the banks flattered me on my business plan, and many said they had never seen one quite as well done. But this was followed by, "We only finance new car dealers, but we wish you well on your new enterprise." It was a familiar story, I concluded. The banks only lend money to the people who don't need the money.

I was taken aback a bit but recharged by the rejection. *Hell, I've been down more difficult roads than this. Besides, I've got great credit and credit card companies love me.* Within a month, I had enough credit lines to buy as many cars as I needed; all I had to do was sell them and pay them off quickly. This really got Dianne's anxiety level rising, but her faith never wavered. We were car dealers.

Even though it took until April to start selling cars, on January of 1996 we were licensed as Gene Gorman and Associates Inc., dba Gene Gorman Auto Sales.

chapter 46

Gene Gorman Auto Sales

om Wright, my former agent and business manager, and I had stayed close over the previous year and a half. Once I got licensed, he asked if there was anything he could do in Florida to help me get set up. I told him I would need a lot of help getting things arranged the way I liked them, and because he was familiar with my style of business, he could come down from Virginia and join me. I assured him I could pay him well but he would have to get his own place to live. He decided to make a trip down and evaluate the possibilities. Within a week, he was on the scene. After surveying the operation, he asked if he could set up house in the back of one of our buildings.

The former parts building used to have an apartment in the back room that was now used for storage but had a kitchen and bathroom as well as a living area and small bedroom. It was ideal for anyone who wanted to take the time to do a bit of decorating. Tom was a wizard at that, and within a week he had himself quite a neat little apartment. Now, how about getting rid of all those toilets and refrigerators.

Once I had everything in place and Tom had himself a comfortable lifestyle, it was time to go buy some cars. In my analysis, I noticed that no one in my market had any imports. I reasoned that with my background in selling imports, this might be a niche I could capture while my competitors were sleeping. Gene Gorman Auto Sales could stock about thirty cars comfortably, so I went to the nearest auction and stocked up on Toyotas, Hondas, and Nissans, with a few domestic cars just to fill up the vacant spaces on the lot. Yep, I was going to be the new import king. With my expertise and Tom's loyalty, I figured we should hit the ground running.

After sixty days, we still had all of those imports, and the only cars we were selling in little old Punta Gorda were the domestic cars. Even though my research had shown the other dealers were selling primarily domestic cars—Chevys, Fords, and tons of Chrysler products—I had foolishly supposed I could make a market where none existed. This was one of the many lessons learned in the first year.

The problem was that most of our market was made up of retirees, and they were still very anti-import. The younger markets like Virginia Beach didn't have the Pearl Harbor resentment that these old folks had. Now I knew why our competitors didn't carry any imports. Before long, I was taking the imports back to the auction to be bought by dealers from the younger markets of Florida like Orlando, Tampa, Miami, and Jacksonville.

I then stocked up on Chrysler Fifth Avenues and all of the Mercury Grand Marquis cars I could find. Once filled with the right inventory, business took off and my old competitive spirit came back. Then I set out to discover what the top guys' numbers were.

In order to not make the same mistake I made in the beginning, I decided I would invest in a monthly report that showed exactly what every dealer, new and used, was selling within twenty-five miles of my market and carry the hottest-selling products. It became an invaluable report, and I use it to this day. By the end of the first year, we were the number-one-selling independent dealer in our county, selling more used cars than almost all of the new car franchises. Interestingly enough, the banks started seeking my business and making me proposals. This has held true for the past eighteen years but not without some interesting challenges along the way.

After considerable begging on my part, Dianne became our comptroller, and I decided to use the slogan, "I'd give 'em away, but my wife won't let me." I picked it up from a guy in California called "Mad Man" Earl Muntz. It seemed apropos for our structure and was a huge hit in our marketplace. I also decided I would put my picture on all of our signs so people would know there was a live human being they could talk to if they had a problem. I felt that would be a plus when people were buying a used car. In addition, I believed it created a relationship with everyone in the community who drove by our dealerships. In the first few years, while our kids were very active in school sports and clubs, their friends would comment, "Oh, your mom is the one that won't let your dad give 'em away," and customers would invariably say to me, "Let me talk to your wife." The slogan was and is a big part of our local identity.

chapter 47

Gratitude in Abundance

After Owen graduated from high school, he went on to Edison State College and Florida Gulf Coast University to study psychology. He had been a large part of our company in the last couple years of high school, handling all of the inventory and detailing needs, but he wanted to go on to college. I encouraged him to follow his dreams and said that if he wanted to become part of the business, it would be here for him.

After completing his education and finding out that he really loved the car business, he told me that he wanted to learn everything he could about the money-making end of the business. He caught on quickly to buying and appraising cars, and before long I felt it was time to send him to the highly acclaimed "Jim Moran" finance and insurance school.

It was a demanding school but necessary for anyone who plans on moving up in the car business. He was by far the youngest guy in the class and had no experience in finance, but his gift was always numbers. Furthermore, he grew up in the car business, so he knew more about the overall business than most of the people in the class, in spite of his youth. He became one of the class stars. I was extremely proud of him. He immediately went to work buying most of our cars. Within a couple more years, he had bought some property and a nice home and had a beautiful redheaded wife named—believe it or not—Aimee. That made three people whose names sounded like "Amy" in our family. It could sometimes get confusing.

Chad had gone on to the University of Florida on an academic scholarship. He wanted to be a medical doctor, so all of his courses were geared toward the sciences and other anatomical and biological "stuff." Sometimes he would come home to visit, and I would look at his books, not having a clue what I was looking at. I thought, *Obviously, this boy got his mama's brains.* He graduated from American University of the Caribbean Medical School and then went on to the University of Oklahoma Medical Center in Oklahoma City to do his residency. What a great experience it was for Dianne and me to go to St. Maarten in the Caribbean to visit Chad. It is a beautiful island with a gorgeous medical school campus. On one of our visits, Dianne and I cooked Thanksgiving dinner for about twenty students. They were ecstatic that folks from the States would do this for them, and we became temporary Mom and Dad to all of them.

When he graduated and walked to the stage, the whole family was in the audience with a huge banner reading "Wonder Boy." We yelled it out as he took his diploma. It's very common for new doctors to be part of a family of doctors, but no one in our family had ever become a doctor. The whole family was beaming. When we went to restaurants on the island after graduation, the other parents and students would shout out "Wonder Boy!" upon seeing him enter.

After his residency, Chad went on to do a sports medicine fellowship, and finally, after twelve years of school beyond high school, he was ready to practice medicine. By then, he was a board certified MD in family practice as well as sports medicine.

One of the great happenings occurred early in his residency— he met the love of his life. Amanda was not only a brilliant woman; she also happened to be beautiful. She was an attorney for the local state appeals court and, according to Chad, "She's a lot smarter than me." They shared the same basic values. She was from a family similar to ours, and Dianne and I couldn't wait to meet her.

On our first night out in Oklahoma City, we went to a cigar bar. Chad and I liked to smoke a good cigar as we talked over the problems of the world, the Florida Gators, the various miracles in our lives, and just about anything that needs to be fixed. We were enjoying being together as we sat in the bar waiting for the owner to bring us the latest selection of fine, overpriced cigars.

Much to my surprise, Dianne and Amanda sat and suffered through the pain of smoke without complaining, and Amanda eventually smiled and, not to be outdone by us guys, lit one up for herself. Dianne was not to be swayed, but it told me a little something about this lady of his. She seemed comfortable in her own skin, and I could see why he was attracted to her.

After all of the various graduations, Chad secured a great job as the sports medicine doctor for an orthopedic practice in Brooksville, Florida, a small town just north of Tampa and only ninety miles north of Punta Gorda. He and Amanda moved to north Tampa in August of 2013. She took the Florida bar, passed, and was immediately hired by the State Appeals Court of Florida. They were married in April of 2014.

chapter 48

Friday, August 13, 2004: Hurricane Charley Pays a Visit

B y 2004, we were well on our way to having our best year ever. We had repeatedly increased our volume and profit by approximately 20 percent each year. One of our newest ventures was adding a new location about a hundred yards down from our original one, and we called it Gorman Family Motors. In 2001, we had started financing some of our own cars rather than putting the contracts with a bank or a small loan company. In many places, this is referred to as Buy Here Pay Here, or BHPH. As in most communities, a certain segment of the people were in need of a reliable car at a fair price but were burdened by bad credit in their past, and no banks would touch them.

The small loan companies would charge ridiculous interest rates, and that never sat well with me. I had been in these customers' positions in the past. I thought I could do better for them and at the same time make a fair profit.

Our interest rates were sometimes 10 percent less than they

could get anywhere else, and that made me feel good. Since most of these folks were families, I thought the name "Gorman Family" might make them feel more comfortable. It seemed to work because it caught on instantly. We financed the cheapest cars we sold, but most of them had warranties and had been checked out extensively to ensure that they would keep running. People with bad credit would pay if the car kept running. Most people with bad credit were good people who had fallen on hard times or had made some bad decisions in their past and were now trying to get back on their feet. I guess you could say we were trying to help people yet still make some money. Business was good at both of our locations, and we were optimistic about the future.

On Friday, August 13, 2004, a Category 4 hurricane ripped through our community and literally destroyed the town. Hurricane Charley was supposed to go north toward Tampa, but because of the sudden shift in the wind current, it took a hard right turn and tore through Punta Gorda before heading inland and going north. The eye of the storm passed directly over our neighborhood and business community with winds in excess of 170 miles per hour. Both of our car lots were destroyed, and the inventories at both locations were devastated by wind and debris.

About half of our cars were totaled, and the remainder suffered massive damage. In addition, every home in the town was terribly damaged, with roofs torn off as well as windows and frames completely warped and twisted. Some homes were leveled. My son Jason, who was visiting at the time, was home with me, and we watched as our roof disappeared, windows and doors were bent and twisted by the pressure, and our lanai was torn off to be carried away to someplace still unknown. Owen was at his home with his fiancée, Aimee, and they suffered the same consequences. Power lines were down everywhere, and we went without power for about ten days. Fortunately, Dianne was in Virginia when the storm hit, and Chad was at the University of Florida in Gainesville.

When the storm finally passed, Jason and I got in a four-wheel-drive truck I had taken home and started working our way toward the dealerships to survey the damage. We figured we would check a few of the surrounding retirement neighborhoods to see if anyone needed any emergency help before we headed to the car lots. Some of the seniors were walking around in shock, but no one needed our help.

When we got to the dealerships, it was obvious we were going to be out of business for a long time. As we walked around the back of the sales office, a tender moment occurred. It suddenly hit me that all of this work we had done for so many years was gone in a flash. I stood there surveying the damage and became overwhelmed with sadness at the lost homes of my employees as well as the hard work that seemed to have been all for naught.

I broke down and started sobbing. Jason came to my side, put his arm around my shoulder, and without saying anything, just stood there consoling his dad. We had had our difficulties over the years, but when it came down to the wire, my eldest son, whom I had abandoned years before, was there beside me. I'll never forget that moment.

There were no working phones anywhere, but somehow Dianne managed to get me a message that she would be flying into Fort Myers the next day and asked if I would pick her up. As we left the airport, I tried to avoid letting her see the devastation as long as I could. We drove all around surveying the damage of the town until I finally had to take her to her office. She was awestruck when we got there. As she walked around the grounds, there wasn't much to say other than my weak attempt to let her know that things would be okay. A few of the guys had come in to offer whatever help they could; there really was nothing we could do but start salvaging what was salvageable. There was about three feet of water in the remnants of each of the buildings, and all the records and paperwork were pretty much destroyed.

We always flew an American flag and a Marine Corps flag outside of the main entrance, and we had taken them down when we knew the storm was coming. They were somewhere inside the building, scattered among the floating debris. As the guys and I were standing outside trying to come up with a plan, Dianne suddenly came out of the building and we watched as she walked past us, saying, "I'm going to stick this somewhere."

She walked all the way to the front of the car lot carrying the American flag. She looked around for a place to stick it and found a piece of chain link fence that had blown in from someplace and plunged the flagpole into the ground, using the fence to stabilize it. Being a Marine I thought, my God she's having her own little Iwo Jima moment. I looked at the guys and smiled. No victims in this family, I can assure you. We knew everything was going to be okay.

I had a business meeting with the entire team, about twenty-five people, within a day or two after the storm and assured all of our employees that we would do all we could to keep them working; we would understand, however, if they needed to make life changes because of the disaster. Giving them a place to work and stay busy seemed to be therapeutic for them because no one left. They were all anxious to get to rebuilding. I was proud of our team, and they inspired me to come up with a plan to get things back on track quickly. How do you get back to business after a devastating storm destroys everything you have? It's really quite simple. You just keep moving piles of debris from one spot to another until it's your turn to have the dump trucks come by and get it.

The morning after the hurricane, I went to my regular 8:00 a.m. recovery group meeting to survey the damage to the church. It had pretty much been destroyed. About thirty people were wandering around looking for a place to meet. After sifting through the debris for chairs, we had our meeting in the parking lot among fallen trees and various forms of construction rubble; the topic for the meeting was—you guessed it—gratitude. In recovery groups, you learn to find the good in everything, no matter how hard you have to look.

*

For the first two weeks, we worked amid the debris in our garage. I then purchased a small trailer to work out of, and we eventually worked our way up to two large trailers and a rebuilt garage. I had salvaged a few old three-part buyers' orders, and Dianne had found the necessary paperwork to be legal, so, even though there was no power, we would be able to sell cars if we had a customer or two.

People were going to need cars—that's for sure—but their insurance checks would be backlogged and payments would be slow in coming. We had excellent insurance, and within two weeks the beleaguered agent arrived at our location, walking around every car or its remains and shaking his head. When he was done, he handed me a bank draft, which of course is money in the bank. I'll bet he didn't say ten words the entire two or three hours he was at our location. I looked at the draft and then looked at him and said, "What do you want me to do with all of these cars now that you've paid me for them?" He said, "Mister, they're yours now, and I don't care what you do with them. I got ten thousand cars to appraise and get rid of. Some guy from Kansas will be coming around if you want to sell them to him." And off he went.

As fate would have it, three more hurricanes followed over the next six weeks. Frances, Ivan, and Jeanne each slowed down any recovery progress, and it was only after mid-September that we could get started on any real rehab for our business.

*

The national media, of course, was all over this story. Water and food trailers were everywhere, and a Realtor from Naples erected a meal tent on a condo sales location in Punta Gorda. When Dianne and I went there for a hot meal on day two after the storm, we were surprised to see my old friend Al Speach, an old Norview High School buddy and Pi Delta Pi brother. He was there with his wife, Terry, who had gone to school with Dianne. It felt good to have that connection at this challenging time. The Federal Emergency Management Agency (FEMA) was on the scene providing help, and a virtual city of FEMA trailers was set up just outside of town.

There was talk of available unemployment dollars for those affected by the storm. Dianne and I both agreed we would not seek help. We still had money in the bank, and for some strange reason the idea of claiming victimhood when we both were still capable of working was out of the question. Many people were not as fortunate and needed help. Sadly, as is usually the case, many nonvictims took advantage of the system. Most of the local homeless were now housed in FEMA trailers and were living better than they had before the storm. But we wanted to keep our heads high and get to work.

The problem was that it would be impossible to get any repair or body work done on the cars that were still sellable. All of the shops within fifteen miles had been destroyed as well. Somehow, we had to get the damaged inventory out of the way so we could get some fresh inventory. The totaled cars were moved to the back to wait for the guy from Kansas, but we had a lot of damaged yet well-running stuff sitting on the ground that we could sell.

After brainstorming with the team, it hit me. We had done well with our insurance check, and now we owned all the cars for nothing. My sales staff was usually paid 20 to 30 percent of the profit on a deal. Here's an example: As most dealers do, we buy a car from the auction for $10,000 and use our bank credit line, called floor plan, to buy the car. We then sell it for $12,000. We make $2,000, and the salesperson gets 20 percent of the $2,000. We then pay the bank back the $10,000 we borrowed to buy the car in the first place along with a charge for using the money. Well, when we got the insurance draft, we made our profit and paid back the bank for all the cars. But then we had all the cars, and we owned them outright.

Most of them still ran well, but they had body, light, and window damage from flying debris and interior water damage from rain. Of course, many would have to be sold with salvage titles, but that didn't seem to bother most of the bargain hunters. Using a phrase that had gotten some recent exposure from Saddam Hussein, I took out ads in surrounding town newspapers and radio spots advertising "The Mother of All Scratch and Dent Sales." The radio spot said something like this: "Come buy a car from Charlotte County's Number One Used Car Dealer, with a bit of hurricane damage for half price or less. Take it to your own body shop for the minor body work." It was amazing how many people we attracted who wanted to somehow be connected to the hurricane. I just couldn't understand it. I envisioned little old men sitting in their clubs saying, "Well, I got to go now. Got to get my car to the body shop for hurricane damage." And I could hear their friends saying, "Wow, were you in that hurricane?"

The sale was a tremendous success. We got a lot of national automotive publication exposure primarily because we maintained a positive attitude and had not bought into the victim mentality. We all had our health, we were able to work, and we did.

*

Our salespeople really loved the sale because they were now getting 20 to 30 percent from a cost of zero. In the end, the first full month back in business after Hurricane Charley hit our town turned out to be the best profit month in our company's history.

And we cleared out our old stuff and were ready to make the rest of 2004 successful. We would just have to do it in trailers.

I thought about the story of the difference between a pessimist and an optimist. It seemed to me that if you're willing to pray, work hard, and no matter what head toward what seems to be the next right thing to do, somehow you can find a pony in what looks like a pile of horse manure.

chapter 49

Business Is Booming Again

It didn't take long for things to get rolling along pretty well. We would have to wait a while to rebuild, but with strong faith that showing up and doing the next right thing would direct us in the right direction, we had somehow adjusted and were doing as well in the trailers as we had been before Charley roared through.

We knew we were going to miss some of the deals from the Gorman Family location, so after a year, we started looking for a new location in our neighboring town of Port Charlotte. Demographically, it was more of a blue-collar town than Punta Gorda and a lot of our BHPH business came from there before Gorman Family was leveled.

We came across a good spot and, after some intense negotiating, opened our second location about two miles away from our original spot. It worked out perfectly.

There were a few obstacles we had to overcome before rebuilding Gene Gorman Auto Sales, and it looked like we might be in trailers for quite some time. The county had put new code and zoning requirements in place for any buildings destroyed by the hurricane, so it would be impossible to rebuild like we originally had things set up. Foreseeing a long delay, I decided to look for another spot in Punta Gorda. There was a dealer down the road from us who had somehow escaped being totally destroyed. After he had remodeled his place, I noticed that his inventory was shrinking, usually a sign that the dealers is getting ready to close. I stopped by and said, "If you ever run across anyone who has a place like yours that might be interested in getting out of the business, be sure to let me know." Within two weeks, he called, and two weeks after that, we moved our Gene Gorman Auto Sales location into his totally refurbished, "like new" car lot. We had the trailers moved out. We now had two dealerships and two vacant lots.

Within another year, the county softened its stance on codes a bit, and we were able to build a brand new building on our original site. All we had to do then was decide what we were going to do with it. We decided to create another low-price car lot since that demand was growing. After debating with Dianne and Owen on what to call it, I decided to just flaunt the fact that these were going to be inexpensive cars; I chose Gene Gorman's Dirt Cheap Cars.

Since our slogan has always been "I'd give 'em away, but my wife won't let me" coupled with my picture on every sign, I offered Owen the chance to put his name and picture on the Dirt Cheap location's signs. I'll never forget his comment: "So you want me to put my picture on the Dirt Cheap location? I'm out." We laughed, and I agreed to put my mug on that sign as well. Our reputation in the community was our strongest attribute, so we figured we should take advantage of it with all of our locations.

We had been paying outside mechanic shops to do all of our service work for the past eleven years, and when one of our shops decided to close, rather than buy all the high-tech computers necessary to fix modern-day vehicles, we decided to open our own service center in Punta Gorda, right next to our Dirt Cheap location. We then did the same thing in Port Charlotte when the Goodyear Tire store right next to our Gorman Family location was closing. By 2008, we had three dealerships and two service centers, and business was booming all around us. Within another year, we had started our own finance company and warranty company to give us the ability to treat people how they ought to be treated regardless of their financial conditions.

In 2008, the economy started its slide downhill. Many of our employees were nervous about the future because of all of the media buzz and the general "woe is me "mentality circulating around the country. I assured all of our people that I had been through this stuff before and mentioned a recession many years before during the Carter administration that saw interest rates hit 22 percent with double-digit inflation. Most of them had been babies at that time and couldn't believe it. I then told them that we were not going to be participating in the recession; we were just going to work harder and smarter than we ever had before.

I had learned that negativity feeds on itself, and we were going to stay positive and not give negative energy the power to get us down. We had a few slow months, but after adjusting our attitudes as a company, we went on to enjoy a very successful year.

One of the moves I made in 2008, as a bit of corporate leveraging, was to open a dealership in Virginia Beach, my old stomping grounds. I figured that this strong military market was not going to suffer since most of the potential customers there weren't in the stock market or heavily invested in 401(k) plans, which seemed to be evaporating rapidly.

The move came with its own learning curve but turned out to be a very positive investment for us as a company. This also gave me a chance to reconnect with some of my old friends in the Virginia Beach recovery community as well as family members who still lived up there.

I personally spent the entire year up there to get things off the ground. I felt that since it was a totally new operation, I had better set it up personally as I was familiar with the market. Not surprisingly, Owen ran the entire operation in Florida like a fine watch in my absence. The boy just never ceased to amaze me with his business savvy. Dianne would visit monthly for the much-desired hugs and kisses, and things ran well. Life was good.

*

Another of my special bonuses during this time was the chance to watch Amy Gorman run her dance studio. She had been in business for a number of years and was remarkable as a teacher and choreographer.

Each year at her annual recital, she invited me to emcee the event. I had a chance to see my little brown-eyed angel in action as she managed the show featuring seventy-five to a hundred dancers in over thirty numbers. Her stern yet patient method of getting these students, aged three to eighteen years old, to perform always amazed me. In addition, I had a chance to revisit my ex-wife and all of her relatives at these recitals and was always gratified at their continued acceptance of Dianne and me in their presence. Kitty still loved me madly, and in fact we all became good friends—a true miracle.

I also got my annual dose of high school wrestling by watching my grandson, Gabe, become an All-American just as his father and two uncles had. Dianne also was a wrestling fanatic and would come up for all of the big tournaments.

Amy Marie and her kids were doing well. She had become a general contractor as she and her husband, Pat, opened their own construction company. They had two children of their own, Katie and Hunter, to join beautiful Brittany from Amy's previous marriage to make their family complete. In fact, Amy chose to have Hunter born on my birthday, September 5, and I always told him that only the real "cool" guys were born on September 5. We have become very close over the years, and we have traveled to museums and other historical military sites together. He has since become a bit of a history buff like his grandpa. At this writing, he is eleven years old, and his favorite TV channel is the *Military History Channel.* "That Hitler was a bad man, wasn't he, Grandpa?" he asked once. I concurred.

chapter 50

The Next Generation

When Katie was eighteen months old, she was visiting us in Florida and it was discovered that she has type 1 diabetes. As a normal routine, she has had to endure pricking her finger five to eight times a day to check her blood and taking two or three injections each day. In addition, she had to learn that she couldn't eat what the other kids could eat and had to constantly monitor herself throughout the day. This will go on for the rest of her life unless a cure is found. Amazingly, she took on a somewhat angelic personality, never asking for much and generally accepting things as they were. I was blown away by her acceptance and attitude. These were certainly unusual traits for any youngster. I thought she was an angel from some foreign land.

This motivated Dianne and me to take on the Juvenile Diabetes Research Foundation as our family's favorite charity, and each year we have a local golf tournament in Virginia Beach called The Katie's Kup that generates thousands of dollars for research into this debilitating illness. When we first started the tournament, I found myself at another crossroads regarding my ego. Should we do it or not, I wondered, knowing it's going to bring a lot of attention our way, and then I thought, *Maybe it is one of those "God nudges" I get every now and then.* The fact is that it just seemed like the right thing to do.

My latest pride and joy at this writing is my three-year-old grandson, Chase Gorman. Chase is Jason and his girlfriend Shana's little boy. One of my most gratifying moments was when he was born. I was at the hospital with Dianne and was the first one to hold him after his mom and dad. That really touched Jason, and he got very emotional. I was taken aback at first but then remembered not being there when he was born. I too got very emotional; it was a beautiful moment.

I try to pick Chase up at least once a week to go to the gym or a park to do some cool stuff. We usually end up at McDonald's for some free roaming around and pancakes. I love to watch the raised eyes of the seniors as he wanders aimlessly throughout the restaurant, with safety and courtesy as my guidelines. They seem to love his free spirit. Every now and then he will come back to our table, grab a hunk of pancake, and then go back to "checking things out."

My dad passed this year, and I had the chance to see a wise and courageous man go out with dignity to wherever heroes go. One of my golf buddies who read the obituary asked me how it felt to be the new family patriarch. I said I hadn't thought about it but that I guess God and I can handle anything that comes our way. *Patriarch*—now there's another one of those miracles.

chapter 51

The Journey Continues

As I think back over the years, I can't help but be overwhelmed with gratitude. So many people have helped me along the highways of my life. Without the recovery community and the help of mentors like Harold, Pete, Ernie, Jack Horner and of course Tom Wright, and many others, I wouldn't be alive. They constantly kept me centered and taking life one day at a time. In addition, there is no way I could ever have achieved any success, financial or otherwise, without their constant guidance. It is so easy to sound "Pollyanna" about people who have helped along the way, but if you have read this memoir, you know that is definitely true in my case.

While I don't push my beliefs on anyone and respect everyone's right to believe or not believe as they choose, I am so grateful that my mentors, friends, and children have helped me evolve into a more open-minded student of spiritual forces. I often ponder the logic of believing or not believing in God. To those who feel too smart, sophisticated, or "cool" to believe in God, I offer this: I was lost, and after surrendering my life to a power greater than myself and hitting my knees with this prayer—"God, if you do exist, I need help"—my life changed to what you have read.

After working with many people in recovery and outside of

recovery, it becomes obvious that those who have faith in a God that is more powerful than they and that pray to that God have a better and more stress-free life than those who don't. If that is true, how smart, sophisticated, or cool is it to refuse to consider believing in God?

There is also no way I would have ever completed this writing without the support of my wife, Dianne, who kept urging me to put my life on paper for the next generation and anyone else who may find it interesting or perhaps helpful.

My CPA tells me we are doing well financially, and I am grateful for that, but looking back at my adventures, some filled with pain and many filled with comical consequences, I am left with only one wish at this writing. For the remainder of my life, I just want to be a good man. That would be enough.